OUTSMART THE
TAXMAN

"20 LEGAL STRATEGIES TO REDUCE YOUR TAXES"

BY:

BOB CROSS

Disclaimers

This publication is designed to provide accurate and authoritative information regarding the subject matter covered. It is sold with the understanding that neither the author nor the publisher is engaged in rendering legal, investment, accounting, tax or other professional services. While the publisher and author have used their best efforts in preparing this book, they make no representations or warranties with respect to the accuracy or completeness of the contents of this book and specifically disclaim any implied warranties of merchantability or fitness or a particular purpose. No warranty may be created or extended by sales representatives or written sales materials. The advice and strategies contained herein may not be suitable for your situation. You should consult with a professional when appropriate. Neither the publisher nor the author shall be liable for any loss of profit or any other commercial damages, including but not limited to special, incidental, consequential, personal or other damages.

Copyright 2024

No portion of this book may be reproduced in any form without written permission from the publisher or author, except as permitted by U.S. copyright law.

Dedication

This book is dedicated to my wife, Beth, and my family. Thank you for your support in all my crazy endeavors, your endless love, and encouragement. Your belief in me is often more than my belief in myself and has been my greatest strength and inspiration. This book would not have been possible without you all by my side.

Acknowledgements

To my Children: Ashley, Joshua, Chelsea, Corbin and Cash: You make me the proudest father alive. Your presence in my life inspires me to be the best I can be every day.

To my Mentors: There are too many to list: You have been my mentors whether you know it or not. All your guidance and wisdom have shaped me into the Enrolled agent and person I am in this business today. Thank you all for showing me the way.

Get your $297 tax analysis FREE with your book purchase:

Head to my website: www.allcountytaxservices.com and set some time on my calendar for a free 30-minute call to get the process started.

This isn't just about the tax tips. It's about reclaiming your peace of mind by proactively getting into compliance and staying out of the IRS spotlight.

Important Notice:

While every effort has been taken to ensure that the information contained herein is accurate as of the time of publication, tax laws and regulations are constantly changing.

This book is designed to provide active and authoritative information regarding the subject matters covered, but it is sold with the understanding that the publisher is not engaged in rendering legal or accounting services, and no information contained herein should be construed as legal, tax, accounting, or financial advice.

If legal advice or other expert assistance is required, the services of a competent professional person should be sought. The publisher does not guarantee or warrant that readers who use the information provided in this publication will achieve results like those discussed.

Please consult with your tax, legal, or accounting professional for your specific situation.

Contents

Disclaimers i
Dedication iv
Acknowledgements v
INTRODUCTION ix
Chapter 1: 1
Understanding the Tax Landscape 1
Chapter 2: 7
Maximizing Deductions: The Basics 7
Chapter 3: 13
Business Expense Deductions 13
Chapter 4: 22
Personal Deductions and Credits 22
Chapter 5: 29
Tax-Advantaged Retirement Accounts 29
Chapter 6: 37
Health Savings Accounts (HSAs) 37
Chapter 7: 44
 Real Estate Tax Strategies 44
Chapter 8: 51
 Investment Tax Strategies 51
Chapter 9: 57
Small Business Tax Structures 57
   Sole proprietorship vs. LLC vs. S-Corp 57
   Tax implications of each structure 60
Chapter 10: 65

Timing Income and Expenses 65

Chapter 11: 70

Family Tax Planning 70

Chapter 12: 76

Tax Credits for Individuals 76

Chapter 13: 83

Tax Credits for Businesses 83

State and Local Tax Strategies 90

Chapter 15: 96

Tax-Efficient Charitable Giving 96

Chapter 16: 103

Estate Planning and Taxes 103

Chapter 17: 109

International Tax Considerations 109

Chapter 18: 116

Tax Planning for the Self-Employed 116

Chapter 19: 124

Advanced Tax Reduction Strategies 124

Chapter 20: 130

Staying Compliant and Avoiding Audits 130

Conclusion 138

About the Author 140

INTRODUCTION

Did you know that the average American household pays over $15,000 in taxes each year? That's a staggering amount, and for many, it feels like an unavoidable burden. But what if there were legal ways to reduce that number significantly? Welcome to "Outsmart the Taxman: 20 Legal Strategies to Reduce Your Taxes," a comprehensive guide that will revolutionize the way you think about and approach your tax obligations.

In a world where taxes seem to be an ever-increasing part of our financial lives, understanding how to navigate the complex tax landscape has never been more crucial. This book is not about cheating the system or finding loopholes; it's about empowering you with knowledge and strategies to make the most of the tax code's legal provisions. By doing so, you can keep more of your hard-earned money while fully complying with all tax laws and regulations.

As an expert in tax law and financial coaching, I've spent years helping individuals and businesses optimize their tax situations. Through this experience, I've come to realize that there's a significant gap between what most people know about taxes and what they could know to their benefit. This book is my attempt to bridge that gap, providing you with knowledge typically reserved for high-priced tax professionals.

"Outsmart the Taxman" stands out from other tax guides because it doesn't just tell you what to do – it explains why and how. We'll delve into the intricacies of the U.S. tax system, dispel common myths, and provide you with actionable strategies that you can implement immediately. Whether you're a wage earner, a small business owner, or an investor, this book has something valuable to offer you.

Throughout the pages of this book, we'll explore several key themes that are crucial to understanding and optimizing your tax situation. First, we'll focus on the importance of education and awareness. Many people overpay on their taxes simply because they're unaware of the deductions and credits available to them. By the end of this book, you'll have a comprehensive understanding of the tax landscape and the tools at your disposal.

Second, I emphasize the power of strategic planning. Taxes shouldn't be something you think about only once a year when it's time to file. We'll show you how to incorporate tax planning into your year-round financial decisions, potentially saving you thousands of dollars in the process.

Third, we explore the concept of tax efficiency across various aspects of your financial life. From your investment portfolio to your retirement accounts, from your business structure to your charitable giving, I show you how to make choices that minimize your tax burden while aligning with your financial goals.

Fourth, we'll delve into the importance of proper documentation and compliance. While the strategies in this book are designed to help you pay less in taxes, they're all completely legal and above-board. We'll teach you how to keep meticulous records and stay on the right side of the law while maximizing your tax savings.

Lastly, we discuss the value of professional advice. While this book will give you a strong foundation in tax strategy, it also helps you understand when it might be beneficial to seek the help of a tax professional for more complex situations.

This book is written for a wide range of readers, from young professionals just starting their careers to retirees looking to optimize their fixed incomes. It's for small business owners trying to navigate the complexities of business taxation, and for investors seeking to minimize the tax impact on their portfolios. If you earn income, pay taxes, and want to keep more of your money, this book is for you.

By reading "Outsmart the Taxman," you'll gain a new perspective on taxes. Rather than viewing them as an unavoidable burden, you'll begin to see the tax code as a set of rules that, when properly understood and applied, can work in your favor. You'll learn how to identify opportunities for tax savings in your everyday financial decisions, how to structure your affairs for maximum tax efficiency, and how to confidently navigate complex tax situations.

You'll discover strategies for maximizing deductions, both in your personal life and in your business if you have one. We'll explore often-overlooked deductions that could save you hundreds or even thousands of dollars each year. You'll learn about the power of tax-advantaged accounts, from traditional and Roth IRAs to Health Savings Accounts, and how to use them to secure your financial future while reducing your current tax burden.

For those involved in real estate, we dive into specific strategies for property owners and investors, including how to make the most of depreciation, how to utilize 1031 exchanges, and how to take advantage of the capital gains exclusion on your primary residence.

Investors will find a wealth of information on tax-efficient investing strategies, including tax-loss harvesting, managing capital gains, and optimizing dividend taxes. We'll also explore more advanced strategies like oil and gas investments and opportunity zone investments for those looking to take their tax planning to the next level.

Business owners will benefit from our in-depth analysis of different business structures and their tax implications. We'll help you understand the pros and cons of sole proprietorships, LLCs, and S-Corporations, and guide you in choosing the most tax-efficient structure for your specific situation.

Throughout the book, we also address special situations that many taxpayers face. We cover family tax planning, including strategies for maximizing credits and deductions related to dependents and education. We explore tax considerations for the self-employed, including how to manage quarterly estimated taxes and take advantage of special deductions. For those who have international income or assets, we provide guidance on navigating the complex world of international taxation.

But this book isn't just about reducing your tax bill. It's about empowering you to take control of your financial future. By understanding how taxes work and how to minimize them legally, you'll be better equipped to more confidently speak to your tax and financial professional and be able to make informed financial decisions in all areas of your life. Hopefully, with the money you potentially save from your tax bill, you'll be able to plan more effectively for retirement, make smarter investment choices, build more wealth over time, or enjoy the vacation of your dreams.

Moreover, no longer will you feel at the mercy of the tax system or anxious about potential audits. You'll understand your rights and obligations as a taxpayer, and you'll know how to stay compliant while taking full advantage of legal tax-saving opportunities available to you.

As we embark on this journey of tax strategy, I want to emphasize that the goal is not to avoid paying taxes altogether. Taxes are a necessary part of a functioning society, funding everything from infrastructure to education to national defense. The goal, rather, is to pay your fair share – no more, no less. By understanding the tax code and using it to your advantage, you're not cheating the system; you're using it as it was intended to be used.

In the pages that follow, we'll break down complex tax concepts into easy-to-understand language. We'll provide real-world examples to illustrate how these strategies can be applied in your own life. And we'll give you actionable steps you can take to start reducing your tax burden right away.

Remember, every dollar you save in taxes is a dollar you can use to further your own financial goals – whether that's saving for retirement, investing in your business, funding your children's education, or simply enjoying a higher quality of life. By the time you finish this book, you'll have the knowledge and tools to potentially save thousands of dollars each year in taxes.

So, are you ready to outsmart the taxman? Are you prepared to take control of your tax situation and keep more of your hard-earned money? If so, turn the page and let's begin our journey towards tax efficiency and financial empowerment. The strategies you're about to learn could change your financial life forever.

Let's get started!

Chapter 1

Understanding the Tax Landscape

The United States tax system is a complex and ever-evolving entity that affects every citizen and resident. To effectively navigate this intricate landscape, it is crucial to have a solid understanding of its fundamental principles and mechanisms. This chapter aims to provide a comprehensive overview of the US tax system, dispel common misconceptions, and highlight the importance of legal tax reduction strategies.

The US tax system is primarily based on a progressive tax structure, where individuals and businesses with higher incomes are subject to higher tax rates. This system is designed to distribute the tax burden across the population based on the principle of ability to pay. The Internal Revenue Service (IRS), a bureau of the Department of the

Treasury, is responsible for administering and enforcing tax laws, and collecting on taxes owed.

At its core, the US tax system relies on a self-reporting mechanism. Taxpayers are required to calculate their own tax liabilities and file annual returns. This approach places a significant responsibility on individuals and businesses to understand and comply with tax laws. As former Supreme Court Justice Oliver Wendell Holmes Jr. famously stated, "Taxes are what we pay for civilized society." This quote underscores the fundamental role that taxes play in funding essential government services and programs.

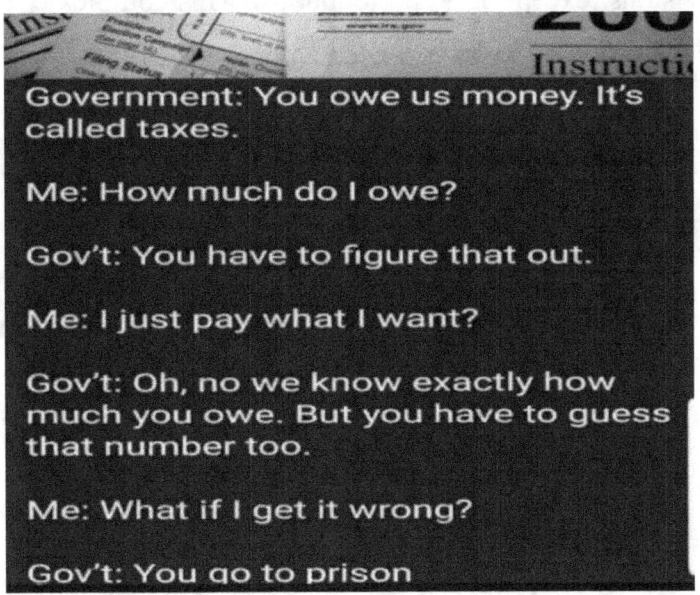

The federal income tax is the largest source of revenue for the US government, but it is far from the only type of tax. Other significant taxes include payroll taxes (which fund Social Security and Medicare), corporate income taxes, estate taxes, and various excise taxes. Each of these tax types has its own set of rules, rates, and regulations, contributing to the overall complexity of the system.

One of the most pervasive misconceptions about taxes is that they are simple and straightforward. The US tax code is notoriously complex, spanning thousands of pages and containing numerous provisions, exceptions, and loopholes. This complexity often leads to confusion and mistakes, even among well-intentioned taxpayers. It's not uncommon for individuals to overpay their taxes simply because they are unaware of deductions or credits for which they qualify.

Another common misconception is that all tax reduction strategies are illegal or unethical. This belief often stems from high-profile cases of tax evasion or aggressive tax avoidance schemes. However, it's crucial to distinguish between illegal tax evasion and legal tax reduction strategies. As Judge Learned Hand famously stated in Gregory v. Helvering (1934), "Anyone may arrange his affairs so that his taxes shall be as low as possible; he is not bound to choose that pattern which best pays the treasury. There is not even a patriotic duty to increase one's taxes."

Legal tax reduction strategies are not only permissible but are often encouraged by the tax code itself. Many tax deductions and credits exist to incentivize certain behaviors or support specific policy goals. For example, deductions for charitable contributions encourage philanthropy, while credits for energy-efficient home improvements promote environmental conservation. Understanding and utilizing these legal strategies is not only smart financial planning but also aligns with the intended purpose of many tax provisions.

The importance of legal tax reduction strategies cannot be overstated. In an increasingly complex economic environment, maximizing after-tax income can have a significant impact on an individual's or business's financial well-being. By implementing effective tax strategies, taxpayers can potentially save thousands of dollars each year, funds that can be redirected towards savings, investments, or other financial goals.

Proper tax planning can help individuals and businesses make more informed financial decisions throughout the year. By understanding how various financial choices impact their tax liability, taxpayers can make strategic decisions that optimize their overall financial position. This proactive approach to tax management can lead to long-term financial benefits and greater fiscal stability.

It's important to note that the tax landscape is not static. Tax laws and regulations are subject to frequent changes, often in response to economic conditions, political shifts, or policy priorities. For instance, the Tax Cuts and Jobs Act of 2017 introduced significant changes to the tax code, affecting everything from individual tax rates to business deductions. Staying informed about these changes is crucial for effective tax planning and compliance.

The complexity of the tax system and the potential benefits of tax planning underscore the value of professional advice. While it's essential for every taxpayer to have a basic understanding of tax principles, working with qualified tax professionals can provide access to specialized knowledge and expertise. Certified Public Accountants (CPAs), Enrolled Agents (EAs), and tax attorneys can offer valuable insights into tax-saving opportunities and help ensure compliance with tax laws.

As we dive deeper into specific tax reduction strategies in subsequent chapters, it's crucial to approach tax planning with a holistic perspective. Effective tax management is not about a single deduction or credit, but rather a comprehensive strategy that considers an individual's or business's entire financial picture. This approach involves understanding how different financial decisions interact with tax laws and how to structure affairs in a tax-efficient manner.

In conclusion, understanding the US tax landscape is the first step towards effective tax management. By dispelling common misconceptions and recognizing the importance of legal tax reduction strategies, taxpayers can take control of their financial future. As we move forward, we will explore a wide range of specific strategies and techniques that can help you navigate the complex world of taxes and ultimately outsmart the taxman – legally and ethically.

As you navigate through this book, each chapter is written as a stand-alone chapter. Not every chapter may apply to you. You can review the table of contents and go directly to the chapter of choice.

Chapter 2

Maximizing Deductions: The Basics

As we move from understanding the broader tax landscape, let's begin with maximizing deductions. This chapter will explore the fundamental strategies that can help you reduce your taxable income and, consequently, your overall tax burden.

Standard vs. itemized deductions form the cornerstone of tax reduction for most individuals. The U.S. tax system allows taxpayers to choose between taking a standard deduction—a fixed amount that reduces your taxable income—or itemizing their deductions. The standard deduction is a no-questions-asked reduction in your taxable income. For the 2024 tax year, the standard deduction is $14,600 for single filers and $29,200 for married couples filing jointly. This amount is adjusted annually for inflation.

Itemized deductions, on the other hand, allow you to list specific expenses that can be deducted from your taxable income. These can include mortgage interest, state and local taxes, charitable contributions, and medical expenses that exceed a certain percentage of your adjusted gross income. The key is to choose the option that gives you the largest deduction. For many taxpayers, especially after the Tax Cuts and Jobs Act of 2017 nearly doubled the standard deduction, taking the standard deduction is often the better choice. However, if your itemized deductions exceed the standard deduction, itemizing will result in greater tax savings.

It's worth noting that the decision to itemize or take the standard deduction isn't always straightforward. As tax expert William Perez points out, "Sometimes, even if your itemized deductions are slightly below the standard deduction, it might be worth itemizing on your federal return if it allows you to itemize on your state tax return where the rules may be different." This underscores the importance of considering both federal and state tax implications in your decision-making process.

One of the most significant advantages of itemizing deductions is the ability to claim a wide range of expenses that are often overlooked by taxpayers. These overlooked deductions can add up to substantial tax savings over time. Similarly, educators can deduct up to $250 for classroom supplies they purchase out of pocket, even if they don't itemize their deductions.

Another commonly overlooked deduction is the state sales tax deduction. If you live in a state with no income tax, or if you made large purchases during the year, you might benefit from deducting state sales taxes instead of state income taxes. This is particularly advantageous for residents of states like Florida, Texas, and Washington, which have no state income tax.

Medical expenses are another area where many taxpayers leave money on the table. While you can only deduct medical expenses that exceed 7.5% of your adjusted gross income, many qualifying expenses are often overlooked. These can include travel expenses for medical care, long-term care insurance premiums, and even home modifications made for medical reasons. As I advise all of my clients, "Keep track of all medical-related expenses throughout the year. You might be surprised at how quickly they add up."

Charitable contributions are a well-known deduction, but even here, many taxpayers fail to maximize their deductions. In addition to cash donations, you can deduct the fair market value of donated goods, as well as mileage driven for charitable purposes. If you've made any out-of-pocket purchases while volunteering for a qualified organization, these can often be deducted as charitable contributions if they were contributed to the organization.

One of the most overlooked deductions is the home office deduction, which has become increasingly relevant in the era of remote work. If you use a portion of your home exclusively for business purposes, you may be able to deduct a percentage of your mortgage interest, property taxes, utilities, and maintenance costs. However, it's crucial to understand the strict requirements for this deduction to avoid raising red flags with the IRS. With the TCJA of 2017, this deduction was eliminated from S Corporation owners.

While maximizing deductions can significantly reduce your tax liability, it's essential to maintain meticulous records to support your claims. The importance of proper record-keeping cannot be overstated. As former IRS commissioner Mark W. Everson once said, "Good record-keeping is the foundation of tax compliance." This sentiment holds true whether you're an individual taxpayer or a business owner.

Implementing effective record-keeping practices is crucial for several reasons. First and foremost, it ensures that you can substantiate your deductions in the event of an IRS audit. The burden of proof is on the taxpayer to support their claims, and without proper documentation, you risk having your deductions disallowed. Moreover, good record-keeping helps you identify all possible deductions, ensuring you don't miss out on potential tax savings.

To maintain effective records, start by creating a system that works for you. This might involve using a dedicated app, spreadsheet, or even a physical filing system. The key is consistency. Make it a habit to record expenses as they occur, rather than trying to reconstruct them at tax time. For receipts, consider using a scanner or smartphone app to create digital copies. Many of these apps can categorize expenses automatically, making it easier to organize your deductions come tax time.

When it comes to specific record-keeping practices, different deductions require different types of documentation. For charitable contributions, for instance, you'll need a written acknowledgment from the charity for any single donation of $250 or more. For business expenses, keep detailed logs of mileage, travel costs, and the business purpose of each expense. For medical expenses, maintain a file of all medical bills, prescription receipts, and insurance statements.

It's also important to retain your records for an appropriate length of time. The IRS generally has three years from the date you filed your return to audit you, but this period extends to six years if you've underreported your income by more than 25%. As a rule, it's wise to keep tax records for at least seven years.

While maximizing deductions and maintaining proper records can seem daunting, the potential tax savings make it well worth the effort. As you become more familiar with the deductions available to you and develop efficient record-keeping habits, you'll find that the process becomes easier over time. Remember, every dollar you save in taxes is a dollar that can be put towards your financial goals, whether that's building an emergency fund, saving for retirement, or investing in your future.

As we conclude this chapter on maximizing deductions, it's important to remember that tax laws are complex and constantly evolving. What works one year may not be the best strategy the next. This underscores the importance of staying informed about changes in tax law and considering professional advice when needed.

Chapter 3

Business Expense Deductions

As we transition from understanding the tax landscape and maximizing basic deductions, we now turn our attention to a critical area for many taxpayers: business expense deductions. This chapter delves into the intricacies of qualifying business expenses, home office deductions, and vehicle and travel expenses, providing you with the knowledge to maximize your tax savings while staying within the bounds of the law.

Qualifying business expenses form the backbone of tax reduction strategies for business owners and self-employed individuals. The Internal Revenue Service (IRS) generally allows deductions for expenses that are "ordinary and necessary" for conducting business. However, the interpretation of these terms can often be subjective and requires careful consideration.

An "ordinary" expense is one that is common and accepted in your trade or business. For instance, a graphic designer purchasing design software would be considered an ordinary expense. A "necessary" expense, on the other hand, is one that is helpful and appropriate for your business, though it need not be indispensable. This could include expenses like professional development courses or industry-specific subscriptions.

It's crucial to understand that personal expenses are not deductible, even if they indirectly benefit your business. The key is to maintain a clear separation between personal and business expenses. This separation becomes particularly important when dealing with items that have both personal and business use, such as a cell phone or a computer.

One effective strategy for maximizing business expense deductions is to meticulously track all potential business expenses throughout the year. This includes keeping detailed records of purchases, maintaining receipts, and noting the business purpose of each expense. By doing so, you'll be well-prepared come tax time and can confidently claim all eligible deductions.

Some commonly overlooked business expenses include bank fees for business accounts, postage and shipping costs, and even a portion of your internet and phone bills if used for business purposes. Don't forget about professional fees paid to accountants, lawyers, or consultants, as these are generally fully deductible.

For many small business owners and self-employed individuals, advertising and marketing expenses can be significant. The good news is that these costs are typically 100% deductible. This includes expenses for business cards, website development and hosting, social media advertising, and traditional forms of advertising like newspaper ads or radio spots.

Another area where many business owners can find substantial tax savings is through the depreciation of business assets. When you purchase equipment, furniture, or other long-lasting items for your business, you may be able to deduct the cost over time through depreciation. In some cases, you might even be eligible for accelerated depreciation methods like Section 179 deductions or bonus depreciation, which allow you to deduct the full cost of qualifying assets in the year of purchase.

It's important to note that meals and entertainment expenses have undergone significant changes in recent years. While entertainment expenses are no longer deductible, business meals remain partially deductible. During 2021 and 2022, to support the restaurant industry during the COVID-19 pandemic, business meals provided by restaurants were 100% deductible. However, that was a temporary measure, and it's crucial to stay informed about current regulations regarding meal deductions.

Now, let's turn our attention to one of the most significant deductions available to many small business owners and self-employed individuals: the home office deduction. This deduction allows you to claim a portion of your housing expenses as a business expense if you use part of your home regularly and exclusively for your business.

To qualify for the home office deduction, you must use a portion of your home as your principal place of business, a place to meet clients or customers, or a separate structure used in connection with your business. The key word here is "exclusively." This means that the area you claim as your home office must be used solely for business purposes. A guest bedroom that doubles as an office, for example, would not qualify.

There are two methods for calculating the home office deduction: the regular method and the simplified method. The regular method involves calculating the actual expenses of your home office. This includes direct expenses, such as painting or repairs made to the specific area, and indirect expenses, which are calculated based on the percentage of your home used for business. Indirect expenses can include mortgage interest, property taxes, utilities, insurance, and depreciation.

The simplified method, introduced by the IRS in 2013, allows you to deduct $5 per square foot of home office space, up to a maximum of 300 square feet or $1,500. While this method is easier to calculate, it may result in a smaller deduction for some taxpayers. It's worth running the numbers both ways to see which method provides the larger deduction.

One common misconception about the home office deduction is that it will automatically trigger an audit. While it's true that improperly claimed home office deductions can raise red flags, a legitimately claimed deduction, supported by proper documentation, should not be a cause for concern. The key is to be honest in your claims and maintain thorough records.

For those who work from home occasionally or don't have a dedicated home office, don't despair. You may still be able to deduct some home-related expenses as "unreimbursed employee expenses" if you itemize deductions. However, these deductions are subject to the 2% floor, meaning you can only deduct the amount that exceeds 2% of your adjusted gross income.

Moving on to another significant area of potential tax savings: vehicle and travel expenses. For many businesses, these can represent a substantial portion of overall expenses, and understanding how to properly deduct them can lead to significant tax savings.

Let's start with vehicle expenses. If you use your personal vehicle for business purposes, you have two options for deducting these expenses: the standard mileage rate method or the actual expense method. The standard mileage rate is simpler and involves multiplying your business miles by the IRS-set rate (which changes annually). For 2024, this rate is 67 cents per mile.

The actual expense method, while more complex, can result in a larger deduction for some taxpayers. This method involves tracking all vehicle-related expenses, including gas, oil changes, repairs, insurance, and depreciation, and then deducting the business-use percentage of these expenses. For example, if you use your vehicle 60% for business and 40% for personal use, you can deduct 60% of your total vehicle expenses.

Regardless of which method you choose, it's crucial to keep accurate records of your business mileage. This includes the date of each trip, the destination, the business purpose, and the number of miles driven. A mileage tracking app can be a valuable tool for maintaining these records.

When it comes to travel expenses, the IRS allows you to deduct ordinary and necessary expenses incurred while traveling away from home for your business. This can include transportation costs (airfare, train tickets, etc.), lodging, meals (subject to the 50% limitation), and incidental expenses like tips and laundry.

One area where many taxpayers stumble is the deduction of expenses for trips that combine business and pleasure. If the primary purpose of your trip is business, you can deduct your travel expenses to and from your destination, even if you engage in some personal activities while there. However, you can only deduct expenses related to the business portion of your trip. For example, if you extend a business trip for a few days of vacation, you can't deduct lodging and meal expenses for those additional days.

It's worth noting that special rules apply to conventions and seminars. To be deductible, these must be directly related to your trade or business, and there must be a specific business purpose for attending. Expenses for conventions held outside North America are subject to additional limitations.

For international business travel, things can get even more complex. Generally, you can deduct all your travel expenses of getting to and from your business destination. However, if your trip is primarily for personal reasons, such as a vacation with some business activities, your travel expenses to and from the destination are not deductible. You can only deduct the expenses directly related to conducting business.

One often overlooked aspect of business travel deductions is the potential to deduct expenses for your spouse or dependents who accompany you on a business trip. While their travel expenses are generally not deductible, there are exceptions. If your spouse or dependent is your employee and their presence on the trip serves a bona fide business purpose, their expenses may be deductible.

As we wrap up this chapter on business expense deductions, it's crucial to emphasize the importance of proper documentation. In the event of an audit, the burden of proof is on you to substantiate your deductions. This means keeping detailed records, including receipts, invoices, and logs detailing the business purpose of each expense.

Remember, the key to maximizing your business expense deductions is to be thorough in tracking your expenses, knowledgeable about what qualifies as a deductible expense, and honest in your reporting. While the goal is to reduce your tax liability, it's essential to do so within the bounds of the law.

If you would like a copy of my white paper that I hand out to businesses in the local chamber of commerce, please reach out to me via my website, www.allcountytaxservices.

Chapter 4

Personal Deductions and Credits

As we transition from exploring business expense deductions, let's delve into the realm of personal deductions and credits that can significantly impact your tax liability. Chapter 4 focuses on three key areas that offer substantial opportunities for tax savings: mortgage interest deductions, charitable contributions, and education-related deductions and credits.

Mortgage interest deductions have long been a cornerstone of personal tax planning for homeowners. This deduction allows taxpayers to reduce their taxable income by the amount of interest paid on their mortgage loans, up to certain limits. The Tax Cuts and Jobs Act of 2017 modified these limits, making it even more crucial for homeowners to understand how to maximize this deduction. For mortgages taken out after December 15, 2017, interest is deductible on up to $750,000 of mortgage debt for married couples filing jointly, or $375,000 for single filers. This applies to both primary residences and second homes. For mortgages that existed before this date, the previous limit of $1 million still applies.

It's important to note that the mortgage interest deduction is only available to those who itemize their deductions. With the increase in the standard deduction under the Tax Cuts and Jobs Act, fewer taxpayers are itemizing. However, for those with significant mortgage interest, itemizing may still be the most advantageous option. To determine if itemizing is right for you, you'll need to compare your total itemized deductions, including mortgage interest, to the standard deduction for your filing status.

Another key consideration is that the mortgage must be secured by the home for the interest to be deductible. This means that home 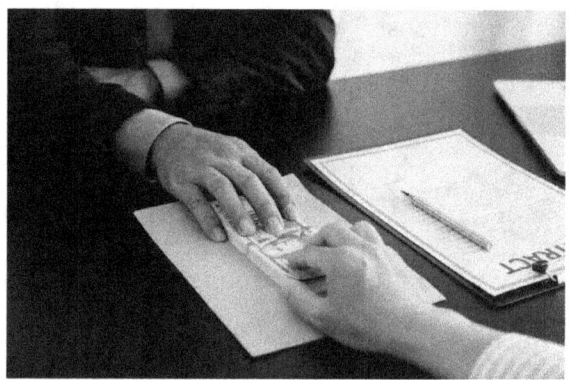 equity loans or lines of credit used for purposes other than buying, building, or substantially improving your home are no longer deductible. This change has led many homeowners to reconsider their borrowing strategies. For example, if you're considering taking out a home equity loan to consolidate debt or pay for a child's education, you should be aware that the interest on such a loan would not be tax-deductible.

For those with high-value homes in expensive real estate markets, the cap on mortgage interest deductions can be a significant factor in tax planning. Some homeowners in this situation have explored strategies such as using a combination of a primary mortgage and a home equity loan to maximize their deductible interest. However, it's crucial to consult with a tax professional before implementing such strategies, as the rules surrounding these deductions can be complex.

Shifting our focus to charitable contributions, we find another powerful tool for reducing tax liability while also supporting causes that are important to you. The IRS allows taxpayers to deduct donations made to qualified charitable organizations, subject to certain limitations. These deductions can include cash donations, donated property, and even out-of-pocket expenses incurred while volunteering for a charitable organization.

For cash donations, you can generally deduct up to 60% of your adjusted gross income (AGI). This limit was temporarily increased to 100% for the 2020 and 2021 tax years as part of COVID-19 relief measures, but has since returned to the 60% cap. For donations of property, the deduction is typically limited to 30%

of AGI, although there are exceptions for certain types of property and organizations.

One strategy that has gained popularity in recent years is the use of donor-advised funds. These funds allow you to make a large charitable contribution in one year, receive the tax deduction immediately, and then distribute the funds to charities over time. This can be particularly useful for taxpayers who experience a high-income year and want to offset their tax liability while spreading out their charitable giving over several years.

Another important consideration is the documentation required for charitable deductions. For any single contribution of $250 or more, you must obtain a written acknowledgment from the charity. For non-cash donations valued at more than $5,000, you'll generally need to obtain a qualified appraisal. Failing to maintain proper documentation can result in the IRS disallowing your deduction, so it's crucial to keep meticulous records of your charitable giving.

When it comes to non-cash donations, it's important to understand how to value the items you're donating. The IRS generally requires that you use the fair market value of the item at the time of donation. For items like clothing and household goods, this is typically much lower than the original purchase price.

However, for items that have appreciated in value, such as stocks or artwork, donating the item directly to charity rather than selling it first can provide additional tax benefits.

Education-related deductions and credits offer another avenue for reducing your tax burden, particularly for families with students in college or those pursuing continuing education. The American Opportunity Tax Credit (AOTC) and the Lifetime Learning Credit are two of the most valuable education-related tax benefits.

The AOTC provides a credit of up to $2,500 per eligible student for the first four years of post-secondary education. To qualify, the student must be pursuing a degree or other recognized education credential and be enrolled at least half-time for at least one academic period during the tax year. The credit is partially refundable, meaning that if the credit brings your tax liability to zero, you can have up to $1,000 of the remaining credit refunded to you.

The Lifetime Learning Credit, on the other hand, is worth up to $2,000 per tax return and is not limited to the first four years of post-secondary education. This credit can be particularly valuable for graduate students or those taking classes to improve job skills.

Unlike the AOTC, the Lifetime Learning Credit is not refundable, but it has no limit on the number of years you can claim it.

It's important to note that you can't claim both the AOTC and the Lifetime Learning Credit for the same student in the same year.

Therefore, it's crucial to carefully evaluate which credit will provide the greatest benefit based on your specific circumstances.

In addition to these credits, there are several education-related deductions to consider. The student loan interest deduction allows you to deduct up to $2,500 of interest paid on qualified student loans. This is an "above-the-line" deduction, meaning you can claim it even if you don't itemize your deductions. However, the deduction phases out for higher-income taxpayers.

For educators, the Educator Expense Deduction allows eligible teachers and other education professionals to deduct up to $250 of out-of-pocket expenses for classroom supplies. This is also an above-the-line deduction, making it particularly valuable for educators who don't itemize.

It's worth noting that the landscape of education-related tax benefits can change from year to year. For example, the tuition and fees deduction, which was once a popular option for many taxpayers, was eliminated after the 2020 tax year. This underscores the importance of staying informed about current tax laws and consulting with a tax professional to ensure you're taking advantage of all available benefits.

As we conclude our exploration of personal deductions and credits, it's clear that these strategies can significantly reduce your tax liability when applied correctly. However, it's equally important to recognize that tax planning is not a one-size-fits-all endeavor. The most effective approach will depend on your individual circumstances, income level, and financial goals.

Chapter 5

Tax-Advantaged Retirement Accounts

As we shift our focus from personal deductions and credits, it's crucial to explore one of the most powerful  tools in the tax-reduction arsenal: tax-advantaged retirement accounts. These accounts not only provide a means to secure your financial future but also offer significant tax benefits that can dramatically reduce your current tax burden.

IMPORTANT NOTE: It is important to note in this chapter that it is written only from a tax standpoint. As an Enrolled Agent, I cannot give out financial planning advice. Please seek the guidance of a licensed Financial Planner.

Traditional vs. Roth IRAs are the cornerstones of individual retirement planning, each offering unique advantages depending on your current financial situation and future expectations. Traditional IRAs allow for tax-deductible contributions, meaning you can reduce your taxable income in the year you make the contribution. This can be particularly beneficial if you're in a high tax bracket and looking for immediate tax relief. For example, if you're in the 24% tax bracket and contribute $6,000 to a traditional IRA, you could potentially save $1,440 in taxes for that year. However, it's important to note that you'll pay taxes on the withdrawals in retirement.

On the other hand, Roth IRAs offer a different kind of tax advantage. While contributions to a Roth IRA are made with after-tax dollars, meaning you don't get an immediate tax deduction, the growth and withdrawals in retirement are completely tax-free. This can be an incredibly powerful tool if you expect to be in a higher tax bracket in retirement or if you believe tax rates will increase in the future. As financial advisor William Bernstein once said, "The Roth IRA is a slam dunk for young workers in low tax brackets who expect to be in higher brackets later in life."

The decision between a Traditional and Roth IRA often comes down to a careful analysis of your current tax situation and your expectations for the future. It's not uncommon for savvy investors to utilize both types of accounts to create tax diversification in retirement. This strategy allows for more flexibility in managing your tax liability during your golden years.

Moving beyond individual retirement accounts, we come to one of the most widely utilized retirement savings vehicles: the 401(k) plan. These employer-sponsored plans allow you to contribute pre-tax dollars directly from your paycheck, reducing your taxable income for the year. The contribution limits for 401(k) plans are significantly higher than those for IRAs, making them a powerful tool for high-income earners looking to shield more of their income from taxes.

One of the most attractive features of 401(k) plans is the employer match. Many companies offer to match a percentage of your contributions, essentially providing you with free money. From a tax perspective, this employer match is even more valuable because it's not counted towards your annual contribution limit. For example, if your employer offers a 50% match on the first 6% of your salary that you contribute, and you earn $100,000 per year, you could contribute $6,000 and receive an additional $3,000 from your employer. This $3,000 is essentially tax-free money that grows tax-deferred in your account.

It's important to understand the vesting schedule for employer contributions. While your personal contributions to a 401(k) are always 100% vested, meaning you own them outright, employer contributions often vest over time. A typical vesting schedule might be 20% per year over five years. This means that if you leave your job before you're fully vested, you may forfeit some of the employer contributions. From a tax planning perspective, it's worth considering this vesting schedule when making career decisions.

For those who are self-employed or run small businesses, the SEP IRA (Simplified Employee Pension Individual Retirement Arrangement) offers a powerful way to save for retirement while reducing current tax liability. SEP IRAs allow for much higher contribution limits than traditional or Roth IRAs, making them an excellent choice for high-earning self-employed individuals.

The beauty of SEP IRAs lies in their simplicity and flexibility. As a self-employed individual, you can contribute up to 25% of your net earnings from self-employment, up to a maximum of $61,000 for 2021 (this limit is adjusted annually for inflation). These contributions are tax-deductible, potentially resulting in significant tax savings in high-income years.

Consider a self-employed consultant earning $200,000 in net profit for the year. They could potentially contribute $50,000 to a SEP IRA (25% of $200,000), reducing their taxable income by that amount. If they're in the 32% tax bracket, this could result in $16,000 in tax savings for the year. As certified financial planner Michael Kitces notes, "For self-employed individuals with high and variable income, the SEP IRA provides an excellent opportunity to make significant retirement contributions in good years, while maintaining the flexibility to contribute less in leaner years."

It's important to note that if you have employees, you generally must contribute the same percentage of their salary to their SEP IRAs as you contribute for yourself. This can make SEP IRAs less attractive for businesses with multiple employees, but for sole proprietors or businesses with few employees, they remain an excellent tax-reduction strategy.

When utilizing any of these tax-advantaged retirement accounts, it's crucial to consider the rules around distributions. For most retirement accounts, including traditional IRAs and 401(k)s, you'll face a 10% early withdrawal penalty if you take distributions before age 59½, in addition to paying income tax on the withdrawal. This penalty is designed to discourage the use of retirement funds for non-retirement purposes.

However, there are exceptions to this rule. For example, first-time homebuyers can withdraw up to $10,000 from an IRA without penalty for a home purchase. Similarly, you can take penalty-free distributions for qualified higher education expenses. Understanding these exceptions can be crucial in your overall financial planning.

On the other end of the spectrum, traditional IRAs and 401(k)s are subject to Required Minimum Distributions (RMDs) starting at age 72. These RMDs are calculated based on your account balance and life expectancy, and failing to take them can result in hefty penalties. From a tax planning perspective, it's essential to factor these RMDs into your long-term strategy, as they can push you into a higher tax bracket in retirement.

Roth IRAs, on the other hand, are not subject to RMDs during the owner's lifetime, providing more flexibility in retirement income planning. This feature makes Roth IRAs an excellent tool for estate planning as well, as your beneficiaries can inherit the account tax-free.

When it comes to maximizing the tax advantages of these retirement accounts, consistency is key. Regular, systematic contributions can help you take full advantage of dollar-cost averaging, potentially lowering your overall investment costs and reducing the impact of market volatility. Moreover, consistent contributions ensure you're continuously reducing your taxable income year after year.

It's also worth considering the impact of fees on your retirement accounts. High fees can significantly erode your returns over time, effectively reducing the tax benefits of these accounts. As

John C. Bogle, founder of Vanguard Group, famously said, "In investing, you get what you don't pay for." When choosing investments within your retirement accounts, pay close attention to expense ratios and other fees.

For those nearing retirement, it's crucial to have a strategy for withdrawing from your various retirement accounts. This is where the concept of tax diversification becomes particularly valuable. By having a mix of pre-tax (traditional), after-tax (Roth), and taxable accounts, you can strategically withdraw from different accounts each year to manage your tax liability in retirement.

For example, in a year where your other income is low, you might choose to do a Roth conversion, moving money from a traditional IRA to a Roth IRA. While you'll pay taxes on the conversion, you may be able to do so at a lower rate than you'd face in the future. This strategy, known as tax bracket management, can significantly reduce your lifetime tax burden.

As we wrap up our discussion on tax-advantaged retirement accounts, it's clear that these vehicles offer powerful opportunities for reducing your current tax liability while securing your financial future. However, the complexity of these accounts and the ever-changing tax laws underscores the importance of working with qualified tax and financial professionals to develop a strategy tailored to your unique situation.'

Chapter 6

Health Savings Accounts (HSAs)

As we transition from our exploration of tax-advantaged retirement accounts in the previous chapter, we now turn our attention to another powerful tool in the tax-saving arsenal: Health Savings Accounts (HSAs). These versatile accounts offer a unique combination of immediate tax benefits and long-term savings potential, making them an essential component of a comprehensive tax reduction strategy.

Health Savings Accounts were introduced in 2003 as part of the Medicare Prescription Drug, Improvement, and Modernization Act. Initially designed to  help individuals with high-deductible health plans (HDHPs) manage their medical expenses, HSAs have evolved into a multifaceted financial tool that savvy taxpayers can leverage for significant tax advantages. As healthcare costs continue to rise and the burden of medical expenses weighs heavily on many Americans, understanding and utilizing HSAs has become increasingly important.

The first key aspect of HSAs that we need to explore is eligibility. Not everyone can open and contribute to an HSA, as there are specific requirements set by the Internal Revenue Service (IRS). To be eligible for an HSA, you must be enrolled in a qualifying high-deductible health plan. For 2023, the IRS defines an HDHP as a plan with a minimum deductible of $1,500 for individual coverage or $3,000 for family coverage. Additionally, the plan must have an out-of-pocket maximum that does not exceed $7,500 for individual coverage or $15,000 for family coverage.

It's important to note that having other health coverage, such as a spouse's non-HDHP plan or a flexible spending account (FSA), can disqualify you from contributing to an HSA. Medicare enrollment also renders you ineligible for new HSA contributions, although you can continue to use funds from an existing HSA to pay for qualified medical expenses.

Age is another factor to consider. While there is no upper age limit for contributing to an HSA, you must be at least 18 years old and not claimed as a dependent on someone else's tax return. These eligibility requirements underscore the importance of carefully evaluating your health insurance options and overall financial situation before deciding to open an HSA.

Once you've determined your eligibility, it's crucial to understand the contribution limits and tax benefits associated with HSAs. The IRS sets annual limits on how much you can contribute to your HSA, and these limits are adjusted periodically for inflation. For 2024, the maximum contribution limit is $4,150 for individual coverage and $8,300 for family coverage. If you're 55 or older, you can make an additional "catch-up" contribution of $1,000 per year.

The tax benefits of HSAs are truly exceptional, offering a rare "triple tax advantage." First, contributions to your HSA are tax-deductible, reducing your taxable income for the year. If your HSA contributions are made through payroll deductions, they're made with pre-tax dollars, providing an immediate tax savings. Second, the funds in your HSA grow tax-free. Unlike a traditional savings account where you'd owe taxes on interest earned, any growth in your HSA – whether from interest, dividends, or capital gains – is not subject to taxation. Finally, withdrawals from your HSA are tax-free when used for qualified medical expenses.

This triple tax advantage makes HSAs a powerful tool for reducing your overall tax burden. Consider this example: If you're in the 24% tax bracket and contribute the maximum $3,850 to an individual HSA, you could save $924 in federal income taxes for the year. When you factor in potential state income tax savings and the long-term growth of tax-free earnings, the benefits become even more substantial.

It's worth noting that these tax advantages extend beyond the current tax year. Unlike flexible spending accounts (FSAs) which typically have a "use it or lose it" policy, HSA funds roll over from year to year. This feature allows you to accumulate a significant balance over time, creating a robust health care nest egg.

The ability to use HSAs as retirement savings vehicles is perhaps one of their most underappreciated aspects. While HSAs are primarily designed for health care expenses, they can effectively serve as an additional retirement account once you reach age 65. After this age, you can withdraw funds from your HSA for any purpose without incurring a penalty. You'll still owe income taxes on withdrawals not used for qualified medical expenses, but this treatment is identical to traditional IRA withdrawals.

This dual-purpose nature of HSAs – serving both current medical needs and future retirement goals – makes them an attractive option for long-term financial planning. Many financial advisors recommend maximizing HSA contributions even if you don't anticipate high medical expenses in the near term. By paying for current medical costs out of pocket and allowing your HSA balance to grow, you can potentially accumulate a substantial tax-free fund for future health care needs or general retirement expenses.

When using your HSA, it's crucial to understand what qualifies as an eligible medical expense. The IRS provides a comprehensive list in Publication 502, but generally, qualified expenses include a wide range of medical, dental, and vision care costs. This includes obvious items like doctor visits, prescription medications, and hospital stays, but also extends to less obvious expenses such as acupuncture, smoking cessation programs, and even certain home modifications for medical reasons.

One strategy to maximize the benefits of your HSA is to pay for current medical expenses out of pocket while keeping thorough records. By doing this and saving your receipts, you give your HSA balance the opportunity to grow tax-free. Then, years or even decades later, you can reimburse yourself for those past medical expenses from your HSA, effectively taking a tax-free distribution. There's no time limit on when you can reimburse yourself for qualified medical expenses, if the expense occurred after you established your HSA.

It's also worth noting that you can use your HSA to pay for the medical expenses of your spouse and dependents, even if they're not covered under your HDHP. This flexibility can be particularly valuable for families managing various health care needs across different insurance plans.

As we look towards the future, it's clear that HSAs will play an increasingly important role in both health care financing and retirement planning. With health care costs projected to continue rising faster than general inflation, the tax advantages and flexibility of HSAs make them an invaluable tool for managing these expenses.

Moreover, as traditional pension plans become increasingly rare and the future of Social Security remains uncertain, the ability to use HSAs as a supplemental retirement savings vehicle becomes even more attractive. The potential for tax-free growth and withdrawals sets HSAs apart from other retirement accounts, offering a unique opportunity to build a tax-advantaged nest egg.

However, it's important to approach HSAs with a strategic mindset. While the benefits are substantial, they require careful planning and discipline to maximize. This includes making informed decisions about health insurance plans, consistently contributing to your HSA, investing the funds wisely, and maintaining meticulous records of medical expenses.

As we conclude our examination of Health Savings Accounts, it's clear that they offer a powerful combination of current tax savings and long-term financial planning potential. Their unique tax advantages, flexibility, and dual-purpose nature make them an essential consideration for anyone looking to optimize their tax strategy and prepare for future health care costs.

Chapter 7

Real Estate Tax Strategies

The realm of real estate taxation is complex and multifaceted, but it also presents numerous opportunities for savvy investors and homeowners to reduce their tax burden legally and effectively.

Real estate has long been considered a cornerstone of wealth creation, and for good reason. Not only does it offer the potential for appreciation and rental income, but it also comes with a host of tax advantages that can significantly impact an individual's overall financial picture. In this chapter, we will explore three key strategies that can help you maximize your tax savings in the real estate arena: rental property deductions, 1031 exchanges, and the capital gains exclusion on primary residences.

Let's begin with rental property deductions, a powerful tool for property investors to reduce their taxable income. When you own a rental property, the IRS allows you to deduct a wide range of expenses associated with managing and maintaining that property. These deductions can substantially lower your tax bill and improve your overall return on investment.

One of the most significant deductions available to rental property owners is depreciation. The IRS recognizes that buildings and their components wear out over time and allows property owners to deduct a portion of the property's value each year to account for this deterioration. Residential rental properties are typically depreciated over 27.5 years, while commercial properties are depreciated over 39 years. This means that if you own a residential rental property worth $275,000 (excluding the value of the land), you could potentially deduct $10,000 per year in depreciation alone.

It's important to note that land is not depreciable, so you'll need to determine the value of the building separately from the land when calculating depreciation. This can typically be done by referring to your property tax assessment or having an appraisal performed.

In addition to depreciation, rental property owners can deduct a host of other expenses. These include mortgage interest, property taxes, insurance premiums, maintenance and repair costs, utilities (if paid by the landlord), and professional fees such as those paid to property managers or accountants. Even travel expenses incurred to check on your rental property or collect rent can be deductible.

However, it's crucial to maintain meticulous records of all these expenses. As tax expert Tom Wheelwright notes in his book "Tax-Free Wealth," "The key to maximizing your tax deductions is keeping good records. Without good records, you're leaving money on the table." This means saving receipts, maintaining a detailed log of your rental-related activities, and potentially using software designed for rental property accounting.

Another often-overlooked deduction for rental property owners is the home office deduction. If you use a portion of your personal residence exclusively for managing your rental properties, you may be able to deduct a percentage of your home expenses as a business expense. This can include a portion of your mortgage interest, property taxes, utilities, and even depreciation on that part of your home.

Moving on to our second strategy, let's discuss 1031 exchanges, also known as like-kind exchanges. This powerful tool allows real estate investors to defer capital gains taxes when selling an investment property and reinvesting the proceeds into another property of equal or greater value.

Named after Section 1031 of the Internal Revenue Code, these exchanges provide a way for investors to roll over their gains from one property to another without immediately triggering a tax liability. This can be an excellent strategy for investors looking to upgrade their properties or diversify their real estate portfolio without taking a significant tax hit.

To qualify for a 1031 exchange, both the property being sold (the "relinquished property") and the property being acquired (the "replacement property") must be held for productive use in a trade or business or for investment. Personal residences do not qualify for 1031 exchanges. Additionally, the replacement property must be identified within 45 days of selling the relinquished property, and the exchange must be completed within 180 days.

It's important to understand that a 1031 exchange doesn't eliminate taxes; it defers them. When you eventually sell the replacement property without doing another 1031 exchange, you'll owe taxes on the deferred gain from the original sale plus any additional appreciation. However, this deferral can be a powerful wealth-building tool, allowing investors to continually trade up to more valuable properties without their profits being eroded by taxes along the way.

As real estate investor and author Brandon Turner puts it, "1031 exchanges are like the turbo button for your real estate investing." By deferring taxes and reinvesting the full proceeds from each sale, investors can potentially accelerate their wealth accumulation significantly.

However, 1031 exchanges are complex transactions with strict rules and timelines. It's crucial to work with a qualified intermediary and consult with a tax professional experienced in these exchanges to ensure compliance with all IRS regulations.

The third strategy we'll explore is the capital gains exclusion on primary residences. This provision allows homeowners to exclude a significant portion of the profit from the sale of their primary residence from capital gains taxes.

Under current tax law, single filers can exclude up to $250,000 of capital gains from the sale of their primary residence, while married couples filing jointly can exclude up to $500,000. This exclusion can result in substantial tax savings, particularly in areas where home values have appreciated significantly.

To qualify for this exclusion, you must have owned and used the home as your primary residence for at least two of the five years preceding the sale. This two-year period doesn't have to be continuous; it can be made up of different periods totaling 24 months within the five-year window.

For example, let's say a married couple purchased a home for $300,000 and sold it seven years later for $900,000. Assuming they meet the ownership and use tests, they could exclude $500,000 of their $600,000 gain, leaving only $100,000 subject to capital gains tax. Depending on their tax bracket, this could save them tens of thousands of dollars in taxes.

It's worth noting that this exclusion can be used repeatedly throughout your lifetime, if you meet the eligibility requirements each time. This makes it a powerful tool for homeowners who may move frequently due to job changes or other life circumstances.

However, there are some limitations to be aware of. If you've claimed the exclusion on another home sale within the past two years, you generally can't claim it again. Additionally, if you use part of your home for business purposes (such as a home office), you may need to recapture depreciation on that portion of the home when you sell.

Real estate expert and author David Greene emphasizes the power of this strategy: "The primary residence capital gains exclusion is one of the best wealth-building tools available to the average American. It's like a tax-free savings account that also provides you with a place to live."

As we conclude our exploration of real estate tax strategies, it's clear that the tax code offers numerous opportunities for property owners and investors to reduce their tax burden. From the myriad deductions available for rental properties to the powerful deferral mechanism of 1031 exchanges and the substantial tax savings possible through the primary residence exclusion, real estate remains a tax-advantaged asset class.

However, it's crucial to remember that tax laws are complex and subject to change. What works today may not be as effective tomorrow, and strategies that are appropriate for one individual may not be suitable for another. As we prepare to dive into investment tax strategies in the next chapter, keep in mind that consulting with qualified tax professionals is essential to developing a comprehensive tax strategy that aligns with your individual circumstances and goals.

Chapter 8

Investment Tax Strategies

As we transition from exploring real estate tax strategies, it's crucial to understand that savvy investors can further optimize their tax positions through strategic management of their investment portfolios. This chapter delves into three key areas of investment tax strategies: tax-loss harvesting, understanding and leveraging the differences between long-term and short-term capital gains, and implementing effective dividend tax strategies.

Tax-loss harvesting is a powerful technique that can significantly reduce an investor's tax liability. This strategy involves selling securities at a loss to offset capital gains realized from other investments. By doing so, investors can lower their overall tax burden while maintaining their desired market exposure. The concept might seem counterintuitive at first – after all, who wants to sell at a loss? However, when executed properly, tax-loss harvesting can be a valuable tool in an investor's arsenal.

To illustrate the power of tax-loss harvesting, consider the following scenario: An investor has realized $10,000 in capital gains from selling Stock A. Later in the same tax year, they notice that Stock B in their portfolio has decreased in value, resulting in an unrealized loss of $8,000. By selling Stock B and realizing this loss, the investor can offset $8,000 of the gains from Stock A, effectively reducing their taxable capital gains to just $2,000. This simple maneuver could potentially save thousands in taxes, depending on the investor's tax bracket and the nature of the gains.

It's important to note that tax-loss harvesting isn't just about selling losing positions. The strategy often involves immediately  reinvesting the proceeds from the sale into a similar, but not "substantially identical," investment. This approach, known as a "wash sale," allows investors to maintain their overall market exposure while still capturing the tax benefits of the realized loss. However, investors must be cautious to avoid running afoul of the IRS's wash sale rule, which disallows the deduction if a substantially identical security is purchased within 30 days before or after the sale.

While tax-loss harvesting can be a powerful strategy, it's not without its complexities. Investors must carefully consider factors such as transaction costs, potential future appreciation of the sold securities, and the impact on their overall investment strategy. As renowned investor Warren Buffett once said, "The first rule of investment is don't lose money. And the second rule of investment is don't forget the first rule." While Buffett wasn't specifically referring to tax-loss harvesting, his wisdom underscores the importance of making investment decisions based on sound financial principles, not solely for tax benefits.

Moving beyond tax-loss harvesting, understanding the distinction between long-term and short-term capital gains is crucial for effective tax planning. The U.S. tax code provides preferential treatment to long-term capital gains, which are realized from the sale of assets held for more than one year. As of 2023, long-term capital gains are taxed at rates of 0%, 15%, or 20%, depending on the taxpayer's income level. In contrast, short-term capital gains, those realized from assets held for one year or less, are taxed as ordinary income, which can result in significantly higher tax rates for many investors.

This disparity in tax treatment creates a strong incentive for investors to hold their appreciated assets for at least one year before selling. For example, consider an investor in the 32% marginal tax bracket who has a $50,000 gain on a stock investment. If they sell the stock after holding it for 11 months, they will owe $16,000 in federal taxes on the gain. However, if they wait just one more month to sell, qualifying for long-term capital gains treatment, their tax bill would drop to $7,500 (assuming a 15% long-term capital gains rate). This simple timing decision results in a tax savings of $8,500.

While the benefits of long-term capital gains are clear, it's important not to let the tax tail wag the investment dog. There may be situations where it makes sense to realize short-term gains, such as when an investor believes a stock has reached its peak value or when rebalancing a portfolio. The key is to weigh the tax implications against other investment considerations and make informed decisions that align with overall financial goals.

Another critical aspect of investment tax strategy revolves around dividend income. Dividends can be classified as either "qualified" or "non-qualified," with significant tax implications for each category. Qualified dividends, which must meet specific criteria set by the IRS, are taxed at the same preferential rates as long-term capital gains. Non-qualified dividends, on the other hand, are taxed as ordinary income.

To take advantage of the favorable tax treatment of qualified dividends, investors should focus on stocks of domestic corporations and certain qualified foreign corporations. Additionally, the stock must be held for more than 60 days during the 121-day period that begins 60 days before the ex-dividend date. By prioritizing investments that pay qualified dividends, investors can potentially reduce their overall tax burden.

However, dividend tax strategy extends beyond simply seeking qualified dividends. Investors should also consider the placement of dividend-paying stocks within their overall portfolio. For taxable accounts, it may be advantageous to focus on stocks with qualified dividends or those with lower dividend yields but higher growth potential. Conversely, high-yielding stocks or those paying non-qualified dividends might be better suited for tax-advantaged accounts like IRAs or 401(k)s, where the dividend income can grow tax-deferred or potentially tax-free in the case of Roth accounts.

It's worth noting that dividend tax strategies can become quite complex, particularly for high-net-worth individuals who may be subject to the Net Investment Income Tax (NIIT). This additional 3.8% tax applies to certain investment income for taxpayers with modified adjusted gross income above specified thresholds. In such cases, it becomes even more critical to carefully manage dividend income and consider strategies such as charitable giving or investment in tax-exempt municipal bonds to mitigate the impact of the NIIT.

As we conclude our exploration of investment tax strategies, it's clear that there are numerous opportunities for savvy investors to optimize their tax positions. From tax-loss harvesting to managing the timing of capital gains and strategically approaching dividend income, these techniques can significantly impact an investor's after-tax returns. However, it's crucial to remember that tax considerations should be just one factor in a comprehensive investment strategy.

It's worth noting that many of the principles discussed here can also apply to business investments. Understanding the tax implications of different business structures can be just as important as managing personal investment taxes, particularly for entrepreneurs and small business owners. The interplay between personal and business tax strategies often creates opportunities for holistic tax planning that can benefit both the individual and their business ventures.

Chapter 9:
Small Business Tax Structures

As a small business owner, choosing the right structure of your business can significantly impact your tax obligations. Chapter 9 discusses the critical topic of small business tax structures, exploring the various options available to entrepreneurs and their respective tax implications.

Sole proprietorship vs. LLC vs. S-Corp

The choice of business structure is one of the most crucial decisions a small business owner can make, with far-reaching consequences for both tax liability and personal asset protection. Let's examine the three most common structures for small businesses: sole proprietorships, limited liability companies (LLCs), and S corporations.

Sole proprietorships are the simplest and most common form of business structure, particularly for single-owned businesses or freelancers. From a tax perspective, a sole proprietorship is a "pass-through" entity, meaning that all business income and expenses are reported on the owner's personal tax return using Schedule C. This simplicity is often attractive to new entrepreneurs, as it requires minimal paperwork and allows for straightforward tax filing. However, this structure also comes with significant drawbacks. As tax expert Barbara Weltman notes, "Sole proprietors are personally liable for all debts and obligations of the business, which can put their personal assets at risk."

The tax treatment of sole proprietorships can be both a blessing and a curse. On the one hand, all business profits are subject to self-  employment tax, which covers both the employer and employee portions of Social Security and Medicare taxes. This can result in a higher overall tax burden compared to other business structures. On the other hand, sole proprietors can deduct 100% of their health insurance premiums as an adjustment to income, which can provide substantial tax savings for those with high healthcare costs.

Limited Liability Companies (LLCs) offer a hybrid approach that combines the simplicity of a sole proprietorship with the personal asset protection of a corporation. From a tax perspective, single-member LLCs are treated as "disregarded entities" by default, meaning they're taxed in the same way as sole proprietorships. Multi-member LLCs, on the other hand, are taxed as partnerships by default. However, one of the key advantages of an LLC is its flexibility in tax treatment. As CPA and tax strategist Mark J. Kohler explains, "LLCs can elect to be taxed as S corporations, potentially saving thousands in self-employment taxes while maintaining the simplicity and flexibility of the LLC structure."

This flexibility allows LLC owners to optimize their tax strategy based on their specific circumstances. For instance, an LLC taxed as an S corporation can pay its owner a reasonable salary, with the remaining profits distributed as dividends. This approach can result in significant savings on self-employment taxes, as only the salary portion is subject to these taxes, while the dividend distributions are not.

S corporations, while more complex to set up and maintain than sole proprietorships or LLCs, offer unique tax advantages that can be particularly beneficial for businesses with substantial profits. Like LLCs, S corporations are pass-through entities, meaning the business itself doesn't pay taxes on its income. Instead, profits and losses are passed through to the shareholders, who report them on their individual tax returns.

The primary tax advantage of an S corporation lies in its ability to minimize self-employment taxes. As mentioned earlier, S corporation owners can pay themselves a reasonable salary, which is subject to payroll taxes, and then take additional profits as distributions, which are not subject to self-employment taxes. This strategy can result in significant tax savings, especially for highly profitable businesses. However, it's crucial to note that the IRS closely scrutinizes S corporations to ensure that owner-employees are paying themselves reasonable compensation. As tax attorney and former IRS attorney Sandy Botkin warns, "If you're not paying yourself a reasonable salary, you're asking for trouble with the IRS."

Tax implications of each structure

Understanding the tax implications of each business structure is crucial for making an informed decision. Let's delve deeper into how each structure affects your tax obligations and potential strategies for minimization.

For sole proprietorships, all business income is subject to both income tax and self-employment tax. As of 2023, the self-employment tax rate is 15.3% on the first $160,200 of net income (adjusted annually for inflation), with 12.4% going to Social

Security and 2.9% to Medicare. Above this threshold, the rate drops to 2.9% for Medicare only, with an additional 0.9% Medicare tax on income over $200,000 for single filers or $250,000 for married couples filing jointly. While this tax burden can be substantial, sole proprietors can deduct half of their self-employment tax on their personal tax returns, which helps to offset some of the cost.

LLCs, when taxed as partnerships or disregarded entities, face similar tax treatment to sole proprietorships. However, the flexibility of the LLC structure allows for more sophisticated tax planning. For instance, multi-member LLCs can allocate profits and losses among members in ways that aren't strictly proportional to ownership percentages, as long as these allocations have "substantial economic effect" as defined by the IRS. This can be a powerful tool for tax optimization among business partners with different tax situations.

When an LLC elects to be taxed as an S corporation, it opens additional tax planning opportunities. The key strategy here is to pay the owner-employee a reasonable salary and take the remaining profits as distributions. Let's consider an example: Suppose an LLC taxed as an S corporation has $200,000 in net income. The owner might pay herself a salary of $100,000, which would be subject to both income tax and payroll taxes. The remaining $100,000 could be taken as a distribution, which would be subject to income tax but not self-employment tax. This strategy could save the owner nearly $15,000 in self-employment taxes compared to a sole proprietorship or LLC taxed as a partnership. S corporations are limited to 100 shareholders, who must be U.S. citizens or residents. They're also restricted to one class of stock, which can limit flexibility in profit distribution. However, for businesses that meet these criteria, the S corporation structure can offer significant tax savings.

It's worth noting that the Tax Cuts and Jobs Act of 2017 introduced a new deduction that benefits many pass-through entities, including sole proprietorships, LLCs, and S corporations. This is the Qualified Business Income (QBI) deduction, also known as the Section 199A deduction. This provision allows eligible taxpayers to deduct up to 20% of their qualified business income from their taxable income. However, the deduction is subject to limitations based on the taxpayer's total taxable income, the type of business, and the amount of W-2 wages paid by the business.

Selecting the optimal business structure involves more than just tax considerations. It requires a holistic evaluation of your business goals, growth plans, liability concerns, and administrative capacity. From a tax perspective, here are some general guidelines to consider:

For new, low-profit businesses or side hustles, a sole proprietorship might be the most straightforward option. The simplicity of tax filing and minimal administrative requirements can outweigh the potential tax savings of more complex structures.

For businesses with moderate profits or those seeking liability protection without complex tax strategies, an LLC taxed as a partnership (for multi-member LLCs) or disregarded entity (for single-member LLCs) could be ideal. This structure offers personal asset protection while maintaining tax simplicity.

For highly profitable businesses or those with significant growth potential, an S corporation or an LLC taxed as an S corporation often provides the most tax advantages. The ability to minimize self-employment taxes through the salary-distribution strategy can result in substantial savings.

It's crucial to remember that your business structure isn't set in stone. As your business grows and evolves, you may find that a different structure becomes more advantageous. Many businesses start as sole proprietorships or simple LLCs and later transition to S corporation status as their profits increase.

Moreover, state-specific considerations can play a role in your decision. Some states, like California, impose additional taxes or fees on certain business structures. For instance, California charges an $800 annual franchise tax on LLCs and corporations, which could influence the decision for small businesses operating in that state.

Ultimately, the choice of business structure is a complex decision that can have significant long-term implications for your tax liability and overall business success. While this chapter provides a foundation for understanding the tax implications of various structures, it's always advisable to consult with a qualified tax professional AND an attorney before making a final decision. They can provide personalized advice based on your specific circumstances and help you navigate the complexities of business taxation.

IMPORTANT NOTE: Choosing the right entity is a legal decision based on the information of an attorney and not a tax professional. A tax professional can only provide information based on potential tax savings for choosing a certain entity.

Chapter 10:
Timing Income and Expenses

The timing of income and expenses can significantly impact your tax liability. This chapter discusses the strategic timing of income recognition and expense deduction, a powerful tool in the arsenal of legal tax reduction strategies.

Income deferral strategies are among the most effective ways to manage your tax burden. The fundamental principle behind income deferral is simple: by pushing income into a future tax year, you can potentially reduce your current year's tax liability. This strategy can be particularly beneficial if you anticipate being in a lower tax bracket in the following year or if you need to balance out a particularly high-income year.

One common method of income deferral is the use of installment sales. When you sell property for a gain, you typically must report the entire gain in the year of the sale. However, if you receive payments over multiple years, you may be able to use the installment method to spread the gain—and the resulting tax liability—over several years. This can be especially useful for business owners selling their companies or real estate investors disposing of properties.

Another income deferral strategy involves delaying billing for services or goods provided near the end of the tax year. For cash-basis taxpayers, income is generally not recognized until payment is received. By sending out invoices in late December rather than early December, you can effectively push that income into the next tax year. However, it's crucial to note that this strategy must be implemented consistently and not merely as a tax avoidance scheme.

For those with more complex financial situations, consider the use of deferred compensation plans. These plans allow you to postpone receiving a  portion of your earned income until a later date, often retirement. While this strategy can be highly effective, it requires careful planning and adherence to strict IRS rules to avoid running afoul of regulations.

On the flip side of income deferral is the strategy of accelerating deductions. The goal here is to recognize expenses in the current tax year to offset income and reduce your tax liability. This approach can be particularly beneficial if you expect to be in a higher tax bracket in the current year compared to future years.

One of the most straightforward ways to accelerate deductions is to pay deductible expenses before the end of the tax year. This could include paying property taxes early, making charitable contributions, or purchasing necessary business supplies and equipment. Remember, for cash-basis taxpayers, expenses are generally deductible when paid, not when incurred.

For businesses, the concept of accelerating deductions often intersects with depreciation strategies. Section 179 of the Internal Revenue Code allows businesses to deduct the full purchase price of qualifying equipment and/or software purchased or financed during the tax year. This can be a powerful tool for reducing taxable income, especially for small businesses making significant capital investments.

Another strategy for accelerating deductions is to bunch itemized deductions. This involves consolidating deductible expenses into a single tax year to exceed the standard deduction threshold. For example, if your itemized deductions are close to the standard deduction amount, you might consider making two years' worth of charitable contributions in a single year to itemize deductions in that year and take the standard deduction the following year.

It's important to note that while these strategies can be highly effective, they must be implemented with care and consideration of your overall financial picture. As renowned tax attorney Robert McKenzie warns, "Taxpayers should be cautious about deferring too much income or accelerating too many deductions if it will create a cash flow problem. The goal is to reduce taxes, not to create financial stress."

Tax-year planning for businesses is another crucial aspect of timing income and expenses. For most businesses, the tax year coincides with the calendar year. However, in some cases, it may be advantageous to elect a fiscal year that doesn't end on December 31. This can be particularly useful for seasonal businesses or those with income and expense patterns that don't align well with the calendar year.

For example, a retail business that experiences its busiest season during the holiday months might benefit from a fiscal year ending January 31. This allows the business to include its peak season in a single tax year, potentially simplifying accounting and tax planning.

When considering a change in tax year, it's crucial to weigh the potential benefits against the complexities involved. Changing your tax year requires IRS approval and can have far-reaching implications for your accounting practices and financial reporting.

As we navigate these strategies, it's essential to remember the words of Judge Learned Hand, who famously stated, "Anyone may arrange his affairs so that his taxes shall be as low as possible; he is not bound to choose that pattern which best pays the treasury. There is not even a patriotic duty to increase one's taxes." This sentiment underscores the legality and, indeed, the wisdom of strategic tax planning.

However, it's equally important to heed the caution of former IRS Commissioner Mark W. Everson, who said, "The tax code has become so complex that it's created a new industry of lawyers and accountants who interpret the code for the rest of us." This complexity underscores the importance of working with qualified tax professionals when implementing these strategies.

As we conclude our discussion on timing income and expenses, it's clear that these strategies can offer significant tax savings when applied correctly. However, they require careful planning, consistent application, and a thorough understanding of your financial situation and future prospects.

Chapter 11

Family Tax Planning

This chapter explores the various strategies and considerations that can help families optimize their tax situation while providing for their loved ones.

Dependency exemptions have long been a cornerstone of family tax planning. While the Tax Cuts and Jobs Act of 2017 suspended personal exemptions through 2025, understanding the concept remains important for future planning and for state tax purposes where applicable. Traditionally, taxpayers could claim a dependency exemption for each qualifying child or relative, reducing their taxable income. The key to maximizing this benefit lies in understanding who qualifies as a dependent. A qualifying child must be under 19 years old (or under 24 if a full-time student), live with the taxpayer for more than half the year, and not provide more than half of their own support. For qualifying relatives, the rules are slightly different, allowing for older dependents who meet certain income and support tests.

It's worth noting that even though personal exemptions are currently suspended at the federal level, the concept of dependency still plays a crucial role in determining eligibility for various credits and deductions. As tax laws are subject to change, staying informed about potential reinstatement of exemptions or new related provisions is essential for effective long-term family tax planning.

The Child Tax Credit is another significant benefit for families with children. This credit has undergone several changes in recent years, making it more valuable for many taxpayers. As of the most recent tax law, the Child Tax Credit provides up to $2,000 per qualifying child under the age of 17. What makes this credit particularly attractive is that it's partially refundable, meaning that even if the credit exceeds the tax owed, families can receive up to $1,400 per child as a refund.

To maximize the benefit of the Child Tax Credit, it's crucial to understand the phase-out limits. The credit begins to phase out for married couples filing jointly with modified adjusted gross income (MAGI) exceeding $400,000, and for all other filers with MAGI exceeding $200,000. Planning your income around these thresholds can help ensure you receive the full benefit of the credit.

It's also important to note that there's an additional credit for other dependents who don't qualify for the Child Tax Credit. This non-refundable credit of up to $500 per dependent can apply to older children or other qualifying relatives. By carefully considering all dependents in your household, you can potentially reduce your tax liability significantly.

Education savings accounts, particularly 529 plans, offer another avenue for tax-advantaged family planning. These plans allow you to save for  your children's or grandchildren's education expenses while enjoying tax benefits. Contributions to 529 plans grow tax-free, and withdrawals are tax-free when used for qualified education expenses. While contributions are not deductible on your federal tax return, many states offer tax deductions or credits for 529 plan contributions.

The power of 529 plans lies in their flexibility and potential for long-term growth. You can change beneficiaries within the family without incurring penalties, allowing you to adjust your savings strategy as family needs evolve. Moreover, with the passage of the SECURE Act, up to $10,000 from 529 plans can now be used to repay student loans for the beneficiary or their siblings.

To maximize the benefits of 529 plans, consider front-loading contributions. The IRS allows you to contribute up to five years' worth of gifts in a single year without incurring gift tax consequences. This strategy can jumpstart the account's growth potential while potentially reducing your taxable estate.

Another consideration in family tax planning is the Kiddie Tax. This provision was designed to prevent parents from shifting large amounts of investment income to their children to take advantage of lower tax rates. Under current law, a child's unearned income over a certain threshold is taxed at the parents' marginal rate. Understanding these rules is crucial when considering investment strategies for your children.

For families with elderly parents or relatives, considering the Medical Expense Deduction can lead to significant tax savings. If you're paying for a dependent parent's medical expenses, these costs can potentially be deductible if they, along with your own medical expenses, exceed 7.5% of your adjusted gross income. This deduction can be particularly valuable for families with high medical costs.

In the realm of family tax planning, it's also worth exploring the benefits of hiring family members in your business. If you own a business, employing your children can be a tax-efficient way to shift income to a lower tax bracket. Children under 18 working for their parents' unincorporated business are exempt from FICA taxes, and their standard deduction can shield a significant amount of earned income from taxation.

The Earned Income Tax Credit (EITC) is another important consideration for lower to middle-income families. This refundable credit can provide a substantial boost to eligible taxpayers, particularly those with children. The amount of the credit varies based on income and the number of qualifying children. Understanding the EITC's parameters and planning your income accordingly can help maximize this benefit.

As we look towards the future, it's important to consider the impact of potential tax law changes on family tax planning strategies. The tax landscape is constantly evolving, and what works today may need to be adjusted tomorrow. Staying informed about proposed legislation and being prepared to adapt your strategies is crucial for long-term success in minimizing your family's tax burden.

In conclusion, effective family tax planning requires a comprehensive approach that considers various credits, deductions, and savings vehicles. By understanding and leveraging these tools, families can significantly reduce their tax liability while providing for their loved ones' needs and future goals.

Chapter 12

Tax Credits for Individuals

Tax credits for individuals are powerful tools that can significantly lower your tax liability, often providing a dollar-for-dollar reduction in the amount of tax you owe. In this chapter, we'll delve into three key tax credits that can make a substantial difference in your overall tax burden: the Earned Income Tax Credit, Residential Energy Credits, and the Adoption Credit.

The Earned Income Tax Credit (EITC) stands as one of the most significant tax credits available to low to moderate-income workers. This refundable credit not only reduces the amount of tax you owe but can also result in a refund if the credit exceeds your tax liability. The EITC was designed to provide financial support to working individuals and families, encouraging and rewarding work. The amount of credit you can receive depends on your income, filing status, and the number of qualifying children you have.

To qualify for the EITC, you must have earned income from employment or self-employment. The credit is particularly beneficial for those with children, but childless workers can also qualify if they meet certain criteria. This substantial tax credit can make a significant difference in a family's financial situation.

However, claiming the EITC requires careful attention to detail. The IRS estimates that about 20% of eligible taxpayers fail to claim this credit, leaving billions of dollars unclaimed each year. On the flip side, the EITC is also subject to a high rate of improper payments, often due to complexity and confusion surrounding eligibility rules. As tax expert John Waggoner notes, "The EITC is one of the most valuable credits available to working Americans, but it's also one of the most misunderstood. It's crucial to check your eligibility each year, as your situation may change."

Moving on to another valuable credit, the Residential Energy Credit offers homeowners an incentive to make energy-efficient improvements to their residences. This credit comes in two forms: the Nonbusiness Energy Property Credit and the Residential Renewable Energy Tax Credit.

The Nonbusiness Energy Property Credit allows homeowners to claim a credit for installing energy-efficient improvements such as insulation, windows, doors, and certain heating and cooling systems. While this credit has been subject to lifetime limits in the past, recent legislation has extended and expanded its availability. It's important to keep abreast of the current rules, as they can change from year to year.

The Residential Renewable Energy Tax Credit, on the other hand, provides a credit for installing renewable energy systems in your home, such as solar panels, wind turbines, or geothermal heat pumps. This credit has been particularly generous, allowing homeowners to claim up to 30% of the cost of these systems. While the credit was originally set to phase out, recent legislation has extended its availability at the 30% rate through 2032.

These energy credits serve a dual purpose: they reduce your tax liability while also encouraging environmentally friendly home improvements. As energy costs continue to rise and climate change concerns grow, these credits become increasingly valuable. They offer a financial incentive to make improvements that can lower your energy bills and reduce your carbon footprint.

It's crucial to maintain detailed records of any energy-efficient improvements you make to your home. Keep receipts, manufacturer certifications, and any other relevant documentation.

These will be essential if you're audited and need to prove your eligibility for the credits.

The third major credit we'll explore in this chapter is the Adoption Credit. This non-refundable credit is designed to help offset the high costs associated with adopting a child. For the 2021 tax year, the maximum credit was $14,440 per child, a substantial amount that can significantly ease the financial burden of adoption.

The Adoption Credit covers qualified adoption expenses, which include reasonable and necessary adoption fees, court costs, attorney fees, traveling expenses, and other expenses directly related to the legal adoption of an eligible child. It's important to note that the credit is subject to income limitations, and it begins to phase out for taxpayers with modified adjusted gross incomes above a certain threshold.

One unique aspect of the Adoption Credit is that it can be claimed before the adoption is finalized, if you've incurred qualified expenses. If you adopt a special needs child, you may be eligible to claim the full credit amount even if your actual expenses were less.

The Adoption Credit can be particularly valuable because it can be carried forward for up to five years if you can't use the full amount in the year you claim it. This feature recognizes that adoption expenses often exceed a family's tax liability in a single year.

As adoption attorney Emily Dudak Taylor points out, "The Adoption Credit is one of the most substantial tax benefits available to adoptive families. It can make a significant difference in making adoption financially feasible for many families. However, it's crucial to understand the rules and keep meticulous records of all adoption-related expenses."

While these three credits - the Earned Income Tax Credit, Residential Energy Credits, and the Adoption Credit - are among the most significant for individuals, they're far from the only credits available. Other credits that may apply depending on your situation include the Child Tax Credit, the Credit for the Elderly or Disabled, the Retirement Savings Contributions Credit (also known as the Saver's Credit), and various education-related credits.

Each of these credits has its own set of rules, income limitations, and documentation requirements. It's crucial to review your situation annually to determine which credits you may be eligible for. Your eligibility can change from year to year based on changes in your income, family situation, or other factors.

One common pitfall in claiming tax credits is assuming that you're ineligible without thoroughly checking the requirements. Tax laws change frequently, and credits that you weren't eligible for in the past may become available to you. Conversely, credits you've claimed in the past may no longer be applicable. This underscores the importance of staying informed about tax law changes and reviewing your situation each year.

Another critical point to remember is that tax credits are more valuable than deductions of the same amount. While deductions reduce your taxable income, credits directly reduce your tax liability dollar for dollar. For example, a $1,000 tax credit saves you $1,000 in taxes, regardless of your tax bracket. In contrast, a $1,000 deduction would save you $220 if you're in the 22% tax bracket.

It's also worth noting that some credits, like the Earned Income Tax Credit, are refundable. This means that even if the credit exceeds your tax liability, you can receive the excess as a refund. Other credits, like the Adoption Credit, are non-refundable, meaning they can reduce your tax liability to zero, but you won't receive a refund for any excess credit.

When claiming tax credits, accuracy is paramount. Errors in claiming credits can trigger audits and potentially lead to penalties. If you're unsure about your eligibility for a particular credit or how to claim it correctly, it's wise to consult with a tax professional. The cost of professional advice can often be offset by the tax savings from correctly claimed credits. Tax preparer penalties for these tax credits are substantial. Be prepared to provide extensive substantiation documents to your tax professional.

As we conclude our exploration of tax credits for individuals, it's clear that these powerful tools can play a crucial role in reducing your overall tax burden. From supporting low to moderate-income workers through the Earned Income Tax Credit to encouraging energy-efficient home improvements and easing the financial challenges of adoption, these credits reflect various social and economic policy goals embedded in our tax system.

Understanding and properly utilizing these credits requires diligence, careful record-keeping, and often, professional guidance. However, the potential tax savings make this effort worthwhile

Chapter 13:
Tax Credits for Businesses

As businesses navigate the complex landscape of tax obligations, it's crucial to understand and leverage available tax credits. These credits can significantly reduce a company's tax liability, freeing up capital for growth and investment. In this chapter, we'll explore three powerful tax credits that businesses should consider: the Research and Development Credit, the Work Opportunity Tax Credit, and the Small Business Health Care Tax Credit.

The Research and Development (R&D) Credit is a valuable incentive designed to encourage innovation and technological advancement in the United States. This credit can be a game-changer for companies investing in new products, processes, or software. The R&D Credit is not limited to large corporations or high-tech industries; businesses of all sizes and across various sectors can potentially benefit from this credit.

To qualify for the R&D Credit, activities must meet four criteria set by the IRS. First, they must be intended to develop new or improved business components, such as products, processes, software, techniques, formulas, or inventions. Second, the activities must involve experimentation. Third, the experimentation must be aimed at eliminating uncertainty about the development or improvement of a business component. Finally, the process must rely on hard sciences such as engineering, physics, chemistry, biology, or computer science.

The calculation of the R&D Credit can be complex, but generally, it's based on qualified research expenses (QREs). These expenses typically include wages for employees directly engaged in R&D activities, supplies used in the research process, and certain contract research expenses. The credit amount is usually a percentage of the increase in a company's QREs over a base amount, which is determined by the company's historical spending on R&D.

One of the most significant recent changes to the R&D Credit came with the PATH Act of 2015. This legislation made the credit permanent and allowed eligible small businesses to use the credit to offset Alternative Minimum Tax (AMT). Additionally, certain startup companies can now use up to $250,000 of their R&D Credit to offset payroll taxes. This change has made the credit much more accessible and valuable to early-stage companies that may not yet have significant income tax liabilities.

It's worth noting that proper documentation is crucial when claiming the R&D Credit. Companies should maintain detailed records of their research activities, including project plans, progress reports, and time tracking for employees involved in R&D. These records can be invaluable in the event of an IRS audit.

Moving on to another significant tax credit, the Work Opportunity Tax Credit (WOTC) provides an incentive for employers to hire individuals from certain target groups who have consistently faced barriers to employment. This credit not only helps businesses reduce their tax burden but also promotes workforce diversity and provides opportunities for often-marginalized groups.

The WOTC applies to wages paid to employees from ten target groups: long-term unemployed individuals, veterans, ex-felons, designated community residents living in Empowerment

Zones or Rural Renewal Counties, vocational rehabilitation referrals, summer youth employees living in Empowerment Zones, Supplemental Nutrition Assistance Program (SNAP) recipients, Supplemental Security Income (SSI) recipients, long-term family assistance recipients, and qualified long-term unemployment recipients.

The amount of the credit varies depending on the target group of the employee and the wages paid to that employee. Generally, the credit is calculated as a percentage of qualified wages paid to an eligible employee during their first year of employment. For most target groups, the credit is 40% of qualified first-year wages for employees who work at least 400 hours, with a lower percentage for employees who work fewer hours.

To claim the WOTC, employers must follow a specific process. First, they must obtain certification that the employee is a member of a target group. This is typically done by submitting IRS Form 8850, "Pre-Screening Notice and Certification Request for the Work Opportunity Credit," to the state workforce agency within 28 days after the eligible employee begins work. Once certified, the employer can claim the credit on their federal income tax return using IRS Form 5884, "Work Opportunity Credit."

It's important to note that the WOTC is a non-refundable credit, meaning it can reduce a company's tax liability to zero, but cannot result in a refund. However, any unused credit can be carried back one year or forward for up to 20 years, providing flexibility in how businesses can utilize this benefit.

The third significant tax credit we'll explore is the Small Business Health Care Tax Credit. This credit was introduced as part of the Affordable Care Act to help small businesses and tax-exempt organizations afford the cost of providing health coverage for their employees. While not as widely applicable as the R&D Credit or the WOTC, this credit can provide substantial savings for eligible small businesses.

To qualify for the Small Business Health Care Tax Credit, an employer must meet several criteria. First, the business must have fewer than 25 full-time equivalent employees (FTEs). Second, the average annual wages of these employees must be less than $56,000 (as of 2021, adjusted annually for inflation). Third, the employer must pay at least 50% of the cost of single coverage for each employee. Finally, the employer must offer coverage through the Small Business Health Options Program (SHOP) Marketplace.

The maximum credit is 50% of premiums paid for small business employers and 35% for small tax-exempt employers. The credit is available to eligible employers for two consecutive taxable years. The amount of the credit phases out gradually for employers with average wages between $27,000 and $56,000 and for employers with the equivalent of between 10 and 25 full-time employees.

One of the advantages of this credit is that it's refundable for tax-exempt employers, meaning that even if the organization owes no taxes, it may be eligible to receive the credit as a refund. For small businesses, while the credit is not refundable, it can be carried back or forward to other tax years.

It's worth noting that employers can still deduct the portion of premiums not covered by the credit. As tax expert John Smith points out, "This can result in significant savings. Not only do you get the credit, but you can also deduct the remainder of the premium costs as a business expense."

To claim the Small Business Health Care Tax Credit, eligible employers must use Form 8941, "Credit for Small Employer Health Insurance Premiums," to calculate the credit. The amount from this form is then reported on the business's income tax return.

While these three credits – the R&D Credit, the Work Opportunity Tax Credit, and the Small Business Health Care Tax Credit – can provide substantial tax savings, it's crucial for businesses to carefully evaluate their eligibility and the potential benefits. Each credit has specific requirements and limitations, and the process of claiming these credits can be complex.

Moreover, tax laws and regulations are subject to change, and the specifics of these credits may be modified in future legislation. As always, it's advisable to consult with a qualified tax professional who can provide guidance based on your specific situation and the most current tax laws.

Chapter 14:

State and Local Tax Strategies

While federal taxes tend to dominate discussions about tax planning, savvy taxpayers understand that significant savings can be achieved by optimizing their approach to state and local taxes as well.

State income tax deduction remains one of the most substantial opportunities for reducing your overall tax burden. The Tax Cuts and Jobs Act of 2017 introduced a $10,000 cap on the state and local tax (SALT) deduction, which includes state income taxes, local income taxes, and property taxes. This cap has made it more critical than ever for taxpayers to strategically plan their state income tax payments to maximize their deduction within these constraints.

One effective strategy for maximizing your state income tax deduction is to time your payments carefully. If you're close to or over the $10,000 SALT cap, consider prepaying your fourth quarter estimated state tax payment in December instead of January. This allows you to claim the deduction in the current tax year, potentially providing a larger benefit if you expect your income to be lower in the following year. However, be cautious of the alternative minimum tax (AMT), as state income tax payments are not deductible under the AMT system.

For high-income earners in states with no or low-income tax, such as Florida, Texas, or Nevada, the sales tax deduction can be a valuable alternative. The IRS allows taxpayers to deduct either state and local income taxes or sales taxes, but not both. In states without income tax, opting for the sales tax deduction is a no-brainer. However, even in states with income tax, some taxpayers may benefit more from deducting sales tax if they've made significant purchases during the year.

To claim the sales tax deduction, you have two options: use the IRS sales tax tables based on your income and location or keep detailed records of all your purchases and deduct the actual sales tax paid. For most taxpayers, using the IRS tables is simpler and often sufficient. However, if you've made large purchases like a car, boat, or home improvements, it may be worthwhile to calculate your actual sales tax paid, as these significant expenses can push your deduction above the standard amount provided by the IRS tables.

When considering the sales tax deduction, it's crucial to keep meticulous records of major purchases. This includes not only the item's cost but also any delivery or shipping charges, as these are often subject to sales tax as well. Additionally, if you live in a state with varying local sales tax rates, ensure you're using the correct rate for each purchase location.

Property tax strategies form another critical component of state and local tax planning. With the $10,000 SALT cap in place, homeowners in high-tax states face new challenges in maximizing their property tax deductions. One strategy to consider is "bunching" property tax payments. This involves paying two years' worth of property taxes in a single year, allowing you to potentially exceed the standard deduction and itemize in that year, while taking the standard deduction in the alternate year.

For example, if your property taxes are typically $8,000 per year, you could pay $16,000 in one year (covering the current year and prepaying the next), then pay nothing the following year. This strategy can be particularly effective when combined with other itemized deductions like charitable contributions.

Another property tax strategy involves challenging your property's assessed value. Many homeowners accept their property tax bills without question, but local assessments can often be inaccurate or outdated. By successfully appealing your property's assessed value, you may be able to lower your property tax bill significantly. This not only reduces your out-of-pocket expenses but also helps you stay under the $10,000 SALT cap, potentially allowing you to deduct more of your state income taxes.

When challenging your property assessment, gather evidence of comparable home sales in your area, recent appraisals, and any factors that might negatively impact your home's value, such as nearby construction or changes in the neighborhood. Many jurisdictions have specific procedures and deadlines for assessment appeals, so be sure to familiarize yourself with your local rules.

For business owners, property tax strategies can be even more impactful. If you own commercial property, consider separating the components of your property for tax purposes. This strategy, known as cost segregation, involves identifying and reclassifying certain building components as personal property or land improvements, which can be depreciated over a shorter period than the building itself. While this primarily affects federal taxes, it can also lead to lower property tax assessments in some jurisdictions.

It's worth noting that state and local tax strategies can vary significantly depending on your location. Some states offer unique tax incentives or deductions that can provide substantial savings. For instance, in some states, contributions to 529 college savings plans are deductible on state tax returns. Other states offer credits for energy-efficient home improvements or for investing in certain industries.

It is important to recognize the interconnectedness of various tax strategies. For example, charitable contributions can be an effective way to offset the limitations imposed by the SALT cap. By carefully timing your charitable donations and combining them with property tax bunching, you can potentially create a more favorable tax situation in alternate years.

Remember, state and local tax strategies are just one piece of the larger tax puzzle. While these strategies can provide significant savings, they should always be considered in the context of your overall financial situation and long-term goals. As tax laws continue to evolve, staying informed and working with qualified tax professionals can help ensure that you're making the most of every available opportunity to reduce your tax burden legally and effectively.

Chapter 15:
Tax-Efficient Charitable Giving

Charitable giving can not only make a positive impact on society but also provide significant tax benefits. Tax-efficient charitable giving is a powerful tool that allows individuals to support causes they care about while simultaneously reducing their tax burden. This chapter will explore various strategies to maximize the tax benefits of charitable contributions, focusing on three key areas: donor-advised funds, qualified charitable distributions, and gifting appreciated assets.

Donor-advised funds have gained popularity in recent years as a flexible and tax-efficient way to manage charitable giving. These investment accounts are specifically designed for philanthropic purposes, allowing donors to make contributions, receive an immediate tax deduction, and then recommend grants to their chosen charities over time. One of the primary advantages of donor-advised funds is the ability to separate the timing of the tax deduction from the actual distribution to charities. This can be particularly beneficial in high-income years when maximizing deductions is crucial.

For example, consider a scenario where an individual experiences a windfall from the sale of a business. By contributing a portion of the proceeds to a donor-advised fund, they can 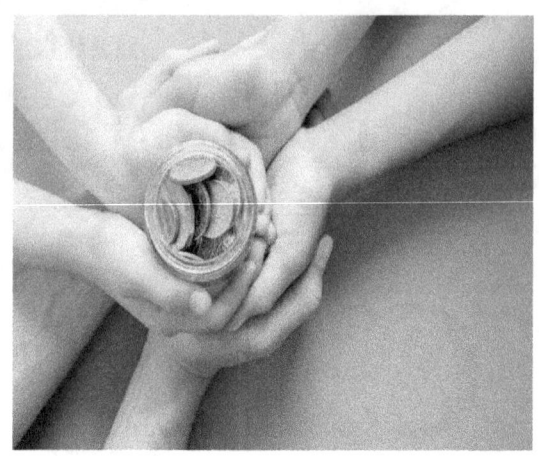 claim a large charitable deduction in the year of the sale, potentially offsetting a significant amount of taxable income. The funds can then be distributed to charities over subsequent years, allowing for thoughtful and strategic giving. As financial advisor Michael Kitces notes, "Donor-advised funds provide a unique opportunity to front-load charitable giving deductions while maintaining long-term control over the actual charitable gifts themselves."

Another key advantage of donor-advised funds is their ability to accept a wide range of assets, including cash, securities, and even certain complex assets like privately held business interests or real estate. This flexibility can be particularly advantageous when dealing with appreciated assets, as we'll explore in more detail later in this chapter.

It's important to note that while donor-advised funds offer significant benefits, they also come with some limitations.

Contributions to these funds are irrevocable, meaning once the assets are donated, they cannot be withdrawn for personal use. Additionally, while donors can recommend grants from the fund, the sponsoring organization has ultimate control over distributions. However, in practice, most reputable donor-advised fund sponsors honor the donor's recommendations as long as they align with the fund's charitable purposes.

Our second strategy, qualified charitable distributions (QCDs) offer a unique opportunity for individuals aged 70½ or older to make tax-efficient charitable contributions directly from their Individual Retirement Accounts (IRAs). This strategy became particularly relevant following the passage of the SECURE Act in 2019, which changed the age for required minimum distributions (RMDs) from 70½ to 72.

QCDs allow eligible individuals to transfer up to $100,000 annually from their IRAs directly to qualified charities. The key benefit of this approach is that the distribution counts towards the donor's RMD for the year but is excluded from taxable income. This can result in significant tax savings, especially for those who don't itemize deductions or are subject to limitations on their charitable deductions.

To illustrate the potential impact of QCDs, consider a retiree with a required minimum distribution of $50,000 who typically donates $10,000 to charity each year. By making a $10,000 QCD instead of taking the distribution and then making a separate donation, they can reduce their adjusted gross income (AGI) by $10,000. This reduction in AGI can have cascading benefits, potentially lowering Medicare premiums, reducing the taxation of Social Security benefits, and increasing eligibility for other deductions and credits that phase out at higher income levels.

It's crucial to note that QCDs must be made directly from the IRA to the qualifying charity. If the funds are first distributed to the account owner and then donated, the tax benefits of the QCD are lost. Additionally, QCDs cannot be made to donor-advised funds, private foundations, or supporting organizations – they must go to public charities.

The third strategy we'll explore is gifting appreciated assets, which can be one of the most tax-efficient ways to support charitable causes. When an individual donates appreciated assets that they've held for more than a year directly to a charity, they can claim a deduction for the full fair market value of the asset while also avoiding capital gains tax on the appreciation.

This strategy can be particularly powerful with highly appreciated securities. For instance, imagine an investor who purchased stock for $10,000 that has since grown to $50,000. If they were to sell the stock and donate the proceeds, they would owe capital gains tax on the $40,000 appreciation. However, by donating the stock directly to a charity, they can claim a $50,000 charitable deduction (subject to AGI limitations) and completely avoid the capital gains tax.

The tax savings from this strategy can be substantial. As tax attorney Robert Wood points out, "Donating appreciated assets is like getting two deductions for the price of one. You deduct the current value and never pay tax on the appreciation." This approach not only maximizes the tax benefit for the donor but also potentially increases the amount received by the charity, as they can sell the asset without incurring capital gains tax.

While gifting appreciated assets is often associated with publicly traded securities, it's worth noting that this strategy can also be applied to other types of property, including real estate, collectibles, and even privately held business interests. However, these more complex assets often require careful planning and valuation to ensure compliance with IRS regulations.

It's important to consider the interplay between these different charitable giving strategies. For example, an individual might use a combination of QCDs for direct gifts to charities, appreciated stock donations to a donor-advised fund for future giving, and cash donations in years when they have high income and can benefit from larger itemized deductions.

When implementing these strategies, timing is crucial. For instance, bunching charitable contributions into a single tax year can help push itemized deductions above the standard deduction threshold, maximizing the tax benefit of the gifts. This approach pairs particularly well with donor-advised funds, allowing for a large upfront deduction while maintaining a consistent giving schedule over time.

It's also worth considering the impact of recent tax law changes on charitable giving strategies. The Tax Cuts and Jobs Act of 2017 nearly doubled the standard deduction, reducing the number of taxpayers who itemize deductions. This change has made strategies like QCDs and bunching donations even more valuable for those looking to maximize the tax benefits of their charitable contributions.

While the tax benefits of charitable giving can be significant, it's crucial to remember that philanthropy should be driven primarily by a desire to make a positive impact rather than solely for tax advantages. As philanthropist Melinda Gates once said, "Philanthropy is not about the money. It's about using whatever resources you have at your fingertips and applying them to improving the world."

In conclusion, tax-efficient charitable giving strategies offer a powerful way to align philanthropic goals with smart tax planning. By leveraging tools like donor-advised funds, qualified charitable distributions, and gifting of appreciated assets, individuals can maximize the impact of their charitable contributions while minimizing their tax burden. Keep in mind that many of these charitable giving strategies can also play a crucial role in comprehensive estate planning, offering opportunities to leave a legacy while managing potential estate tax liabilities.

Chapter 16:
Estate Planning and Taxes

Chapter 16 delves into the intricate world of estate planning and taxes, exploring how individuals can effectively manage their wealth transfer while minimizing the tax burden on their beneficiaries.

IMPORTANT NOTE: Estate planning involves legal advice from an attorney. Tax professionals cannot give legal advice. Seek guidance from qualified attorneys.

Gift tax exclusions form a cornerstone of strategic estate planning. The Internal Revenue Service (IRS) allows individuals to make annual gifts up to a certain amount without incurring gift taxes. As of 2023, this annual exclusion stands at $17,000 per recipient. This means that an individual can give up to $17,000 to as many people as they wish each year without having to report the gifts or pay gift taxes. For married couples, this amount doubles to $34,000 per recipient, as they can split gifts between them. This provision offers a powerful tool for gradually transferring wealth to heirs over time, effectively reducing the size of one's taxable estate.

It's important to note that the gift tax exclusion is separate from the lifetime gift and estate tax exemption. As tax expert Michael Kitces points out, "The annual gift tax exclusion allows individuals to give away substantial amounts over their lifetime without ever touching their lifetime exemption amount." This strategy becomes particularly potent when implemented over many years, allowing for significant wealth transfer without tax consequences.

Beyond the annual exclusion, there are other gift-giving strategies that can help in estate planning. For instance, payments made directly to educational institutions for tuition or to medical providers for health care expenses on behalf of others are exempt from gift taxes, regardless of the amount. This provides an excellent opportunity for individuals to assist family members with substantial expenses while simultaneously reducing their taxable estate.

Another effective strategy involves gifting appreciated assets. When you gift an asset that has appreciated in value, the recipient assumes your cost basis. However, if the recipient's income tax rate is lower than yours, there could be an overall tax saving when the asset is eventually sold. Furthermore, by removing the appreciated asset from your estate, you're also removing its future appreciation, potentially leading to significant estate tax savings down the line.

As of 2023, the federal estate tax exemption was $12.92 million per individual, or $25.84 million for married couples. This means that estates valued below these thresholds are not subject to federal estate taxes. However, it's important to note that this exemption amount is set to sunset at the end of 2025, potentially reverting to a much lower amount unless Congress takes action to extend it.

Given this uncertain future, many high-net-worth individuals are employing strategies to lock in the current high exemption amount. One such strategy is making large gifts now to irrevocable trusts. By doing so, they can utilize the current high exemption amount, effectively removing assets and their future appreciation from their taxable estate. As estate planning attorney Martin Shenkman explains, "Making large gifts now can be a use-it-or-lose-it proposition. If the exemption does decrease in the future, those who have used the higher exemption will have effectively grandfathered in those transfers."

For those with estates that exceed the exemption amount, life insurance can play a crucial role. By setting up an irrevocable life insurance trust (ILIT), individuals can provide liquidity for their heirs to pay estate taxes without the insurance proceeds themselves being subject to estate tax. This strategy requires careful planning and execution but can be immensely beneficial for large estates.

Trusts play a pivotal role in estate and tax planning, offering a myriad of benefits beyond just tax savings. They provide control over how and when assets are distributed, protect assets from creditors, and can ensure the financial well-being of beneficiaries for generations to come. There are numerous types of trusts, each designed to address specific estate planning goals and tax considerations.

One popular trust for tax planning is the grantor retained annuity trust (GRAT). This involves transferring assets to an irrevocable trust while retaining the right to receive an annuity payment for a fixed term. If the assets in the trust appreciate more than the IRS-assumed rate of return (known as the 7520 rate), the excess growth passes to the beneficiaries free of gift tax. As financial planner Robert Keebler notes, "GRATs can be particularly effective in a low-interest-rate environment and for assets expected to appreciate significantly."

Another powerful trust strategy is the intentionally defective grantor trust (IDGT). Despite its somewhat ominous name, an IDGT can be a highly effective tool for estate tax planning. It's structured so that the grantor pays income taxes on the trust's income, effectively allowing the trust assets to grow tax-free. This "tax burn" reduces the grantor's taxable estate while providing a tax-free gift to the trust beneficiaries.

For philanthropically inclined individuals, charitable remainder trusts (CRTs) and charitable lead trusts (CLTs) offer ways to benefit both charities and non-charitable beneficiaries while providing tax advantages. A CRT provides income to the grantor or other beneficiaries for a term of years or for life, with the remainder going to charity. This structure provides an immediate charitable deduction for the present value of the remainder interest. Conversely, a CLT provides an income stream to charity for a term of years, with the remainder passing to non-charitable beneficiaries. This can result in significant gift or estate tax savings.

It's crucial to remember that estate planning is not a one-time event but an ongoing process. Laws change, family situations evolve, and financial circumstances shift. Regular reviews and updates of estate plans are essential to ensure they remain aligned with current laws and personal objectives. As estate planning attorney Ann Levin suggests, "At a minimum, individuals should review their estate plans every three to five years or whenever there's a significant life event or change in tax laws."

Moreover, estate planning extends beyond just tax considerations. It's about ensuring that your legacy is preserved, and your wishes are carried out. This might involve planning for incapacity through documents like durable powers of attorney and advance health care directives. It might also include business succession planning for entrepreneurs or special needs planning for families with disabled dependents.

One often overlooked aspect of estate planning is digital asset management. In our increasingly digital world, consideration must be given to online accounts, cryptocurrencies, and other digital assets. Proper planning ensures that these assets are not lost or inaccessible after one's passing and that they are distributed according to one's wishes.

It's evident that this is a complex field requiring careful consideration and often professional guidance. The strategies discussed here – from gift tax exclusions to various trust structures – offer powerful tools for managing wealth transfer and minimizing tax burdens. However, their effectiveness depends on proper implementation and alignment with individual circumstances and goals.

Chapter 17:
International Tax Considerations

Many individuals find themselves working abroad, investing in foreign markets, or managing international businesses. This chapter will discuss the complex world of international tax considerations, providing you with essential strategies to navigate this intricate landscape.

Foreign earned income exclusion is a crucial concept for American citizens working abroad. This provision allows qualifying individuals to exclude a significant portion of their foreign earnings from U.S. taxation. In 2023, the maximum exclusion amount is $120,000. This exclusion can lead to substantial tax savings for those who meet the eligibility criteria. To qualify, you must meet either the bona fide residence test or the physical presence test. The bona fide residence test requires you to be a resident of a foreign country for an uninterrupted period that includes an entire tax year. The physical presence test, on the other hand, requires you to be physically present in a foreign country for at least 330 full days during a consecutive 12-month period.

It's important to note that the foreign earned income exclusion is not automatic. You must actively claim it by filing Form 2555 with your tax return. Many expatriates overlook this requirement, missing out on significant tax savings. As tax expert Robert Goulder points out, "The foreign earned income exclusion is one of the most valuable tax benefits available to Americans working overseas, yet it's often underutilized due to its complexity and the stringent qualification requirements."

While the foreign earned income exclusion can provide substantial relief, it's not always the most advantageous strategy. In some cases, the foreign tax credit may be more beneficial. The foreign tax credit is designed to prevent double taxation on income earned abroad. It allows you to claim a dollar-for-dollar credit for income taxes paid to a foreign government. This credit can be particularly valuable if you're working in a country with higher tax rates than the United States.

The calculation of the foreign tax credit can be complex, involving various limitations and carryover provisions. It's calculated on Form 1116, which requires detailed information about your foreign source income and the taxes paid on that income. One key advantage of the foreign tax credit over the foreign earned income exclusion is that it can be applied to both earned income and passive income, such as dividends or interest from foreign investments.

In some situations, it may be advantageous to use a combination of the foreign earned income exclusion and the foreign tax credit. This strategy, known as the "splitting" approach, involves claiming the exclusion on a portion of your foreign earned income and then claiming the foreign tax credit on the remainder. This approach can be particularly effective if your foreign earned income exceeds the exclusion amount and you've paid substantial foreign taxes.

As international tax attorney Virginia La Torre Jeker notes, "The decision between the foreign earned income exclusion and the foreign tax credit is not always straightforward. It requires careful analysis of your individual circumstances, including the tax rates in your country of residence, the nature of your income, and your long-term financial goals."

Another critical aspect of international tax planning is the reporting of foreign assets and accounts. The Foreign Account Tax

Compliance Act (FATCA) and the Report of Foreign Bank and Financial Accounts (FBAR) requirements have significantly increased the IRS's ability to track offshore assets and accounts. Failing to comply with these reporting requirements can result in severe penalties, even if no tax is owed.

FATCA requires U.S. taxpayers holding foreign financial assets with an aggregate value exceeding $50,000 to report information about those assets on Form 8938, which is filed with their annual tax return. The reporting threshold varies depending on your filing status and whether you're living in the U.S. or abroad. FATCA also requires foreign financial institutions to report on the assets of their U.S. account holders to the IRS, creating a powerful tool for detecting unreported offshore assets.

The FBAR requirement is separate from FATCA and applies to U.S. persons with a financial interest in or signature authority over foreign financial accounts with an aggregate value exceeding $10,000 at any time during the calendar year. This report is filed electronically using FinCEN Form 114 and is due April 15, with an automatic extension to October 15.

The penalties for non-compliance with these reporting requirements can be severe. For example, the penalty for a non-willful failure to file an FBAR can be up to $10,000 per violation.

For willful violations, the penalty can be the greater of $100,000 or 50% of the balance in the account at the time of the violation.

Given the complexity of these reporting requirements and the potential for substantial penalties, it's crucial to maintain accurate records of all foreign financial accounts and assets. This includes bank accounts, securities accounts, mutual funds, trusts, and even certain insurance policies with a cash value.

For those with more complex international financial situations, such as ownership in foreign corporations or partnerships, additional reporting requirements may apply. For instance, IRS Form 5471 is required for certain U.S. persons who are officers, directors, or shareholders in certain foreign corporations. Form 8865 is used to report interests in foreign partnerships.

It's also important to consider the tax implications of foreign investments. While diversifying your portfolio with international assets can be a sound financial strategy, it can complicate your tax situation. For example, dividends from foreign stocks may be subject to withholding tax by the foreign country. In many cases, you can claim a foreign tax credit for these withholding taxes, but the process can be complex.

Additionally, certain foreign investments can trigger additional tax and reporting requirements. For instance, investments in Passive Foreign Investment Companies (PFICs) are subject to complex and often unfavorable tax rules. PFICs are typically foreign mutual funds or other pooled investments. The tax treatment of PFICs can result in higher tax rates and additional reporting requirements on Form 8621.

As international tax expert Phil Hodgen warns, "PFIC rules are a trap for the unwary. Many U.S. investors in foreign mutual funds are unaware of these rules until they face unexpected tax consequences and reporting requirements."

For U.S. citizens considering renouncing their citizenship for tax purposes, it's crucial to understand the expatriation tax rules. The Heroes Earnings Assistance and Relief Tax (HEART) Act of 2008 introduced the concept of a "covered expatriate," which applies to individuals with a net worth of $2 million or more, or an average annual net income tax liability of more than $171,000 (as of 2023, adjusted annually for inflation) for the five years preceding expatriation.

Covered expatriates are subject to an exit tax, which treats all property of the covered expatriate as if it had been sold for its fair market value on the day before the expatriation date. This can result in a significant tax liability, as the expatriate is required to pay tax on the unrealized gain of their worldwide assets.

Any gifts or bequests from a covered expatriate to a U.S. person are subject to tax at the highest applicable gift or estate tax rate. This provision, sometimes referred to as the "inheritance tax," can have far-reaching consequences for expatriates and their U.S. beneficiaries.

As we conclude our exploration of international tax considerations, it's clear that navigating this complex landscape requires careful planning and expert guidance. The strategies discussed in this chapter – from leveraging the foreign earned income exclusion and foreign tax credit to ensuring compliance with reporting requirements – can help you optimize your tax position in a global context.

Chapter 18:

Tax Planning for the Self-Employed

As we transition from the international tax considerations discussed in the previous chapter, we now turn our attention to a crucial topic for a growing segment of the workforce: tax planning for the self-employed. The gig economy and entrepreneurial spirit have led to an increase in self-employment, bringing with it unique tax challenges and opportunities.

Self-employment offers freedom and flexibility, but it also comes with the responsibility of managing one's own taxes. Unlike traditional employees who have taxes withheld from their paychecks, self-employed individuals must navigate a more complex tax landscape. This chapter will delve into the key aspects of tax planning for those who work for themselves, focusing on quarterly estimated tax payments, self-employment tax deductions, and retirement plans tailored for the self-employed.

Quarterly estimated tax payments are a fundamental aspect of self-employment tax management. When you're self-employed, the burden of ensuring that you pay the right amount of taxes throughout the year falls squarely on your shoulders. The U.S. tax system operates on a "pay-as-you-go" basis, meaning that taxes are due as you earn income. For traditional employees, this is handled through payroll withholdings, but self-employed individuals must take a more proactive approach.

The Internal Revenue Service (IRS) requires self-employed individuals to make quarterly estimated tax payments if they expect to owe $1,000 or more in taxes when they file their annual return. These payments are typically due on April 15, June 15, September 15, and January 15 of the following year. It's crucial to note that these dates can shift if they fall on a weekend or holiday, so always verify the exact due dates for each tax year.

Calculating the correct amount for your quarterly payments can be challenging, especially for those with fluctuating income. A common approach is to estimate your annual tax liability and divide it by four. However, this method may not be suitable for everyone, particularly those with seasonal businesses or irregular income streams. In such cases, the annualized income installment method might be more appropriate. This method allows you to make uneven payments based on your actual income for each period, potentially reducing the risk of underpayment penalties.

Underpayment of estimated taxes can result in penalties, so it's essential to be as accurate as possible. The IRS provides Form 1040-ES to help self-employed individuals calculate their estimated tax payments. This form includes a worksheet that guides you through the process of estimating your income, adjustments, deductions, and credits for the year. While it may seem tedious, taking the time to complete this form can save you from headaches and potential penalties down the road.

It's worth noting that if you also have income from which taxes are withheld, such as a part-time job, you can adjust your  withholdings to cover your self-employment tax liability. This strategy can be particularly useful if you're transitioning into self-employment or if you maintain a part-time job alongside your self-employed work.

Many self-employed persons or those with side hustles do not understand that they are responsible for paying both the employer and employee portions of Social Security and Medicare taxes. This combined tax is known as the self-employment tax, and it can be a significant expense for many self-employed individuals.

The self-employment tax rate is 15.3%, consisting of 12.4% for Social Security and 2.9% for Medicare. This rate applies to your net earnings from self-employment, which is your gross income from your business minus your business expenses. However, there's a silver lining: you can deduct half of your self-employment tax when calculating your adjusted gross income on your tax return.

This deduction is available whether you itemize your deductions or take the standard deduction. It's an "above-the-line" deduction, meaning it reduces your overall taxable income. The reasoning behind this deduction is that it puts self-employed individuals on a more level playing field with traditional employees, for whom employers pay half of these taxes.

To illustrate the impact of this deduction, let's consider an example. Suppose your net self-employment income for the year is $100,000. Your self-employment tax would be $15,300 (15.3% of $100,000). You would be able to deduct half of this amount, or $7,650, from your taxable income. Depending on your tax bracket, this deduction could result in significant tax savings.

It's important to note that while the Social Security portion of the self-employment tax only applies to a certain amount of income (adjusted annually for inflation), the Medicare portion applies to all your net earnings. Additionally, high-income earners may be subject to an Additional Medicare Tax on earnings above certain thresholds.

Beyond the self-employment tax deduction, self-employed individuals have access to a wide array of business expense deductions that can significantly reduce their taxable income. These may include home office expenses, vehicle expenses, travel costs, supplies, professional development, and more. Keeping meticulous records of these expenses is crucial for maximizing your deductions and defending them in case of an audit.

One of the challenges of self-employment is the lack of employer-sponsored retirement plans. However, self-employed individuals have several options for tax-advantaged retirement savings, each with its own benefits and considerations.

The Simplified Employee Pension (SEP) IRA is a popular choice for many self-employed individuals. SEP IRAs are easy to set up and maintain, and they allow for significant contributions. As of 2021, you could contribute up to 25% of your net self-employment income or $58,000, whichever is less. These contributions are tax-deductible, reducing your taxable income for the year. However, SEP IRAs may not be ideal if you have employees, as you're required to make proportional contributions for eligible employees.

Another option is the Solo 401(k), also known as an Individual 401(k). This plan is available to self-employed individuals with no employees other than a spouse. The Solo 401(k) allows for potentially higher contributions than a SEP IRA, as you can make contributions both as an employer and an employee.

The SIMPLE IRA is another option, particularly suitable for self-employed individuals with a few employees. SIMPLE IRAs have lower contribution limits than SEP IRAs or Solo 401(k)s, but they're easier to administer and have lower startup and operating costs.

For those looking to maximize their retirement savings, defined benefit plans are worth considering. These plans, like traditional pension plans, allow for potentially very high contributions based on actuarial calculations. They can be complex and expensive to set up and maintain, but for high-income self-employed individuals looking to make large retirement contributions, they can be an excellent option.

When choosing a retirement plan, it's essential to consider not just the current tax benefits but also your long-term financial goals. Each type of plan has its own rules regarding contributions, distributions, and required minimum distributions (RMDs). Some plans, like Solo 401(k)s, also offer Roth options, allowing for tax-free growth and withdrawals in retirement.

It's also worth noting that contributing to these retirement plans can help reduce your taxable income, potentially lowering your self-employment tax liability as well. This dual benefit makes retirement contributions a powerful tool in your overall tax planning strategy.

As we conclude this chapter on tax planning for the self-employed, it's clear that while self-employment brings unique tax challenges, it also offers numerous opportunities for strategic tax planning. By carefully managing your quarterly estimated tax payments, taking advantage of the self-employment tax deduction and other business deductions, and leveraging tax-advantaged retirement plans, you can significantly reduce your tax burden and build long-term financial security.

Remember, tax laws and regulations are complex and subject to change. While this chapter provides a solid foundation for understanding self-employment tax strategies, it's always advisable to consult with a qualified tax professional for personalized advice tailored to your specific situation. They can help you navigate the intricacies of self-employment taxes and ensure that you're making the most of available deductions and credits.

Chapter 19:
Advanced Tax Reduction Strategies

These methods are not for the faint of heart and often require substantial capital or specific circumstances to implement effectively. However, for those who qualify, they can offer substantial tax benefits that go beyond the more common strategies we've explored in earlier chapters.

Oil and gas investments have long been a favorite of high-net-worth individuals looking to reduce their tax burden. The U.S. tax code provides significant incentives for investing in domestic oil and gas production, primarily to encourage exploration and reduce dependence on foreign energy sources. One of the most attractive features of these investments is the ability to deduct a large portion of the initial investment immediately, often up to 80% in the first year. This deduction is known as Intangible Drilling Costs (IDCs) and can include expenses such as wages, fuel, repairs, and hauling charges related to drilling operations.

The tax benefits don't stop there. After the well starts producing, investors can typically deduct an additional 15% of their income from the well through a provision called depletion allowance. This allowance is designed to compensate for the gradual exhaustion of the oil or gas reserve. It's worth noting that these deductions can often exceed the actual income from the investment in the early years, creating tax losses that can offset other income sources.

However, approach oil and gas investments with caution. As John D. Rockefeller once said, "The oil business is probably the  most speculative in the world." While the tax benefits can be substantial, these investments carry significant risks. The price of oil and gas can be volatile, and there's always the chance that a well may not produce as expected or may run dry sooner than anticipated. Additionally, regulatory changes or shifts in energy policy could impact the profitability of these investments.

For those more inclined towards environmental conservation, conservation easements offer another avenue for significant tax deductions. A conservation easement is a voluntary legal agreement between a landowner and a land trust or government agency that permanently limits the use of the land to protect its conservation values. When you grant a conservation easement, you're essentially giving up certain rights associated with the land, such as the right to develop it, in exchange for substantial tax benefits.

The tax deduction for a conservation easement is based on the difference between the land's value with the easement and its value without the easement. In many cases, this can result in a deduction of 50% or more of the land's fair market value. Moreover, if the property is used for farming or ranching, the deduction can be up to 100% of the donor's adjusted gross income. Any unused deduction can be carried forward for up to 15 years, providing long-term tax benefits.

Conservation easements not only provide tax benefits but also contribute to environmental preservation. As noted conservationist Aldo Leopold once said, "We abuse land because we regard it as a commodity belonging to us. When we see land as a community to which we belong, we may begin to use it with love and respect." This strategy allows landowners to maintain ownership and limited use of their property while ensuring its long-term conservation.

However, it's important to note that the IRS has increased scrutiny on conservation easements in recent years due to some abusive practices. It's crucial to work with reputable land trusts and experienced tax professionals to ensure your conservation easement meets all legal requirements and can withstand potential IRS examination.

Opportunity zone investments represent a more recent addition to the advanced tax reduction toolkit, introduced as part of the Tax Cuts and Jobs Act of 2017. These investments are designed to spur economic development in designated economically distressed communities across the United States. The tax benefits of investing in opportunity zones are threefold: tax deferral, partial tax forgiveness, and potential tax-free growth.

Here's how it works: When you sell an asset that would typically trigger capital gains tax, you can invest those gains into a Qualified Opportunity Fund (QOF) within 180 days. By doing so, you can defer paying taxes on those gains until December 31, 2026, or until you sell your interest in the QOF, whichever comes first. If you hold your investment for at least five years, you'll receive a 10% step-up in basis, effectively reducing your tax liability on the original deferred gain. Hold it for seven years, and that increases to 15%.

But the real magic happens if you hold your investment for at least ten years. In this case, any appreciation on your opportunity zone investment becomes completely tax-free. This potential for tax-free growth on long-term investments is what makes opportunity zones particularly attractive to investors with substantial capital gains.

As with any investment, opportunity zones come with their own set of risks and considerations. These are often long-term, illiquid investments in areas that have historically struggled economically. Success depends not just on the performance of individual projects, but on the overall economic development of the designated zones. As Warren Buffett famously said, "Risk comes from not knowing what you're doing." It's crucial to thoroughly understand the specific opportunity zone, the proposed development projects, and the potential for long-term economic growth in the area before investing.

It's worth noting that these advanced strategies - oil and gas investments, conservation easements, and opportunity zone investments - often require significant capital and come with complexities that demand expert guidance. They're not suitable for everyone and should be considered as part of a comprehensive tax and investment strategy.

While these strategies can offer substantial tax benefits, remember that tax considerations should not be the sole driver of investment decisions. As the saying goes, "Don't let the tax tail wag the investment dog." Each of these strategies should align with your overall financial goals, risk tolerance, and personal values.

By implementing any of these advanced tax reduction strategies, it's imperative to work with experienced tax professionals and legal advisors. The rules surrounding these investments are complex and subject to change. What's more, the IRS often scrutinizes these areas closely, so proper documentation and adherence to all regulations is crucial.

As we look ahead to our final chapter on staying compliant and avoiding audits, it's worth emphasizing that while these advanced strategies can significantly reduce your tax burden, they must be implemented carefully and ethically. The line between tax avoidance (which is legal) and tax evasion (which is not) can sometimes be thin. Always err on the side of caution and full disclosure.

Remember, the goal is not just to reduce taxes in the short term, but to create a sustainable, long-term strategy that aligns with your financial objectives while staying within the bounds of the law. As we'll discuss in the next chapter, maintaining meticulous records and working with qualified professionals are key to successfully implementing these strategies while minimizing the risk of running afoul of the IRS.

Chapter 20:

Staying Compliant and Avoiding Audits

As we conclude our exploration of tax reduction strategies, it's crucial to address the critical aspects of staying compliant with tax laws and minimizing the risk of audits. The Internal Revenue Service (IRS) is vigilant in its efforts to ensure taxpayers are following the rules, and while the strategies we've discussed throughout this book are legal, their improper implementation or documentation can raise red flags. In this final chapter, we discuss the factors that may trigger an audit, the importance of proper documentation, and the benefits of working with tax professionals to ensure you're on the right side of the law while maximizing your tax savings.

Red flags that trigger audits are numerous and varied but understanding them can help you navigate your tax planning with greater confidence. One of the most common triggers is reporting income that doesn't match the information the IRS receives from other sources. For instance, if you fail to report income from a 1099 form, it's likely to catch the attention of the IRS. Similarly, large discrepancies between your reported income and your lifestyle can raise suspicions. If you're claiming a modest income but living in a luxurious home or driving expensive cars, the IRS may want to take a closer look at your finances.

Another red flag is consistently reporting business losses, especially if you're self-employed or run a small business. While it's not uncommon for businesses to experience losses, particularly in the early years, ongoing losses year after year may suggest to the IRS that you're trying to write off personal expenses as business deductions. The agency understands that businesses aim to make a profit, so persistent losses might indicate that your "business" is a hobby, which has different tax implications.

Charitable donations can also attract unwanted attention if they seem disproportionate to your income. While generosity is commendable, the IRS may question large charitable deductions that don't align with your reported earnings. It's essential to keep meticulous records of all donations, including receipts and acknowledgment letters from the organizations you've supported.

Home office deductions, which we discussed in Chapter 3, are another area that the IRS scrutinizes closely. While this deduction can offer significant tax savings for those who qualify, it's also prone to abuse. Claiming an unreasonably large portion of your home as a dedicated office space or deducting expenses that aren't directly related to your work can trigger an audit. Remember, the space must be used exclusively and regularly for your business to qualify for this deduction.

Round numbers on your tax return can also raise eyebrows at the IRS. While it might be tempting to estimate or round off figures, it's always best to report exact amounts. For example, claiming exactly $5,000 in travel expenses or $10,000 in charitable donations may suggest that you're not keeping accurate records and are instead making educated guesses.

High-income earners are naturally more likely to face audits, as the potential for significant tax recovery is greater. If you fall into this category, it's particularly important to ensure that all your deductions and credits are properly documented and justified. The same applies to those with complex tax situations, such as individuals with multiple businesses, international income, or extensive investment portfolios.

Proper documentation practices are your first line of defense against potential audits and your best ally if you do face one. The golden rule of tax documentation is simple: keep records of everything. This includes not just receipts and invoices, but also bank statements, credit card statements, canceled checks, and any other documents that support the income, deductions, and credits you've claimed on your tax return.

For business expenses, maintain a system that clearly separates personal and business transactions. This could involve using separate bank accounts and credit cards for business purposes, or meticulously categorizing expenses in your accounting software. Keep detailed logs for vehicle use, travel expenses, and entertainment costs, noting the business purpose for each expenditure.

When it comes to charitable donations, always obtain and retain written acknowledgments from the organizations you've supported. For non-cash donations, such as clothing or household items, keep detailed lists of the items donated and their fair market value. If you're claiming substantial non-cash donations, consider getting professional appraisals to support your valuation.

For investment-related deductions and credits, maintain records of all transactions, including buy and sell orders, dividend reinvestments, and any fees paid. If you're claiming home office deductions, keep floor plans showing the dedicated office space and records of all related expenses.

It's not enough to simply collect these documents; you need to organize them in a way that makes them easily accessible and understandable. Consider using digital storage solutions that allow you to scan and categorize receipts and documents. Many accounting software packages now offer features that allow you to attach digital copies of receipts directly to transaction records, making it easier to provide comprehensive documentation if needed.

Remember, the burden of proof in tax matters lies with the taxpayer. In the event of an audit, you'll need to substantiate the claims made on your tax return. Without proper documentation, you may find yourself unable to justify deductions or credits, potentially leading to additional taxes, interest, and penalties.

Working with tax professionals can provide an additional layer of protection and expertise in navigating complex tax laws and audit risks. While it's possible to handle your taxes independently, especially if you have a simple tax situation, the benefits of professional assistance often outweigh the costs for those with more complex financial situations or those implementing advanced tax reduction strategies.

A qualified tax professional, such as a Certified Public Accountant (CPA) or Enrolled Agent (EA), brings a wealth of knowledge and experience to the table. They stay up to date with the latest tax laws and regulations, which are constantly evolving. This expertise can be invaluable in ensuring that you're taking advantage of all available deductions and credits while staying within the bounds of the law.

Tax professionals can also provide strategic advice on structuring your finances and business affairs in a tax-efficient manner. They can help you plan for the long term, considering not just your current tax situation but also how your actions today might impact your tax liability in the future. This foresight can be particularly beneficial when it comes to retirement planning, estate planning, or major life changes such as starting a business or investing in real estate.

Tax professionals can also be your advocate in the event of an audit. They can communicate with the IRS on your behalf, explain the rationale behind your tax positions, and help gather and present the necessary documentation. Their familiarity with IRS procedures and requirements can help streamline the audit process and potentially lead to more favorable outcomes.

When choosing a tax professional, look for someone with experience in your specific areas of concern. For instance, if you're a small business owner, seek out a professional with expertise in business taxation. If you have international income or investments, find someone well-versed in international tax law. Don't hesitate to ask potential tax advisors about their qualifications, experience, and approach to staying current with tax laws.

It's important to note that while working with a tax professional can significantly reduce your risk of errors and audits, it doesn't eliminate that risk entirely. You are still ultimately responsible for the information reported on your tax return. Therefore, it's crucial to provide your tax professional with complete and accurate information and to review your return carefully before signing it.

In conclusion, as we wrap up our comprehensive exploration of legal tax reduction strategies, it's clear that the key to successfully minimizing your tax burden lies not just in knowing the strategies, but in implementing them correctly and maintaining impeccable records. The strategies we've discussed throughout this book offer powerful tools for reducing your tax liability, but they must be applied with care and diligence.

Remember, the goal is not to aggressively push the boundaries of tax law, but to take full advantage of the legal opportunities available to you. By understanding the red flags that can trigger audits, maintaining thorough and organized documentation, and working with qualified tax professionals, you can confidently implement tax reduction strategies while minimizing your risk of running afoul of the IRS.

As you move forward in your tax planning journey, keep in mind that tax laws are complex and ever-changing. What works this year may not be as effective next year, and new opportunities may arise. Stay informed, seek professional advice when needed, and regularly review your tax strategies to ensure they align with your current financial situation and goals.

Conclusion

Throughout this book, we've explored a wealth of legal strategies to reduce your tax burden. From maximizing deductions and credits to leveraging tax-advantaged accounts and optimizing business structures, these 20 strategies offer a comprehensive toolkit for individuals and businesses alike. We've dissected the intricacies of personal and business deductions, retirement planning, real estate investments, and charitable giving, all with the goal of helping you keep more of your hard-earned money.

The key takeaway is that proactive tax planning is essential for financial success. By understanding the tax landscape and implementing these strategies, you can significantly reduce your tax liability while remaining fully compliant with the law. Remember, it's not about evading taxes, but rather about making informed decisions that align with your financial goals and take full advantage of the legal opportunities available to you.

As we've seen, tax reduction isn't a one-size-fits-all approach. Whether you're an employee, a business owner, an investor, or somewhere in between, there are specific strategies tailored to your situation. The most effective approach often involves combining multiple strategies and adapting them as your financial circumstances evolve. Stay informed about changes in tax laws and be prepared to adjust your strategies accordingly.

While the world of taxes can seem daunting, the knowledge and strategies presented in this book empower you to take control of your financial future. By outsmarting the taxman legally and ethically, you're not just saving money – you're creating opportunities for growth, investment, and long-term financial stability. Remember, every dollar saved in taxes is a dollar that can be put to work for your future.

Ultimately, the goal is to shift your perspective on taxes from a burdensome obligation to a manageable aspect of your financial life. With the right knowledge and strategies, you can approach tax season with confidence, knowing that you're making the most of every opportunity to reduce your tax liability. Take these lessons to heart, implement the strategies that work best for you, and start outsmarting the taxman today.

About the Author

My name is Bob Cross, Enrolled Agent and Registered Tax Planner.

During my time in the United States Naval Nuclear Power Program, I built my career based on integrity. It was also during this time that as operational commitments would permit, I often volunteered to assist shipmates with their tax preparation in the VITA trailer that the navy provided on base in San Diego. It was something I loved to do and knew that eventually I would return to it after my service ended.

Upon my discharge from the US Navy in 2005, I held various positions in the power plant industry, culminating as a power plant manager operating three power plants in San Diego County where I wrote and managed multimillion dollar per year budgets.

In 2010, while maintaining my full-time employment, I began pursuing my Bachelor of Science in Accounting Degree from the University of Phoenix and graduated in September 2014 at the age of 46. I have also had the pleasure of raising 5 children with my beautiful and supportive wife Beth.

It was during this time attending classes that the desire to return to the tax world returned and again help others with often confusing tax laws. During the summer of 2014 about 3 months before my college graduation, I took the 60-hour California Tax Education Council (CTEC) tax preparer course and became a CTEC Registered Tax Preparer (CRTP), and started All County Tax Services. Additionally, I am registered in the IRS' Annual Filing Season Program and am an authorized e-File Provider.

In January of 2016, I earned my status as an Enrolled Agent, authorized to practice all aspects of taxation before the IRS.

Always trying to improve myself to be better for my clients, in July of 2017, I completed the Business Tax Verified Program through Pronto Tax School. It is an intensive course of instruction to better prepare me for the various business entities including LLC's, C-Corporations, and S-Corporations.

In 2018, I became a Registered Tax Planner. I can assist you in all your tax planning needs, whether you are a business owner or an individual looking for ways to reduce your annual tax bill. If you are in the market to change to your business entity, please give me a call and I can advise you on various pros and cons to find the business entity that will better suit your needs!

As a small veteran owned business, we are available to individual taxpayers, businesses, home-based businesses, and the self-employed. As our client's needs grow, we will continue to grow with them.

When I'm not in the office, I can be found in my BBQ Pit, working around my house, coaching my son's soccer team, camping (glamping), or cruising around on my Harley.

You have my personal guarantee that you will always receive the best possible services, whether you need services ranging from simple 1040, to business tax returns, to complicated Tax Planning.

I don't treat you like a client; I treat you like my family!

Bob Cross

Enrolled Agent

Registered Tax Planner

All County Tax Services LLC

www.ingramcontent.com/pod-product-compliance
Lightning Source LLC
Chambersburg PA
CBHW052319220526
45472CB00001B/183